A CHRISTMAS CAROL

RABBIT ROOM
THEATRE

RABBIT ROOM THEATRE
PRESENTS

A CHRISTMAS CAROL

ADAPTATION BY A. S. PETERSON

from the book
by Charles Dickens

This adaptation of *A Christmas Carol* was developed by Rabbit Room Theatre, directed by Matt Logan, and given its world premiere in Franklin, Tennessee. Performances began December 7th, 2024, at the FSSD Performing Arts Center.

PRODUCTION NOTE

This play makes use of a specific gesture by Scrooge throughout the narrative: that of an arm extended, palm out, as if pushing something away. This gesture is tracked throughout and its development is a key part of Scrooge's character as well as a key part of his final transformation.

Likewise, the character of The Boy, uses an opposite gesture: that of an arm out, palm up, as if welcoming or pleading for help.

CAST

SPIRIT 1 (Lead) - Leader of the company of lesser spirits
SPIRIT 2 - a lesser spirit
SPIRIT 3 - a lesser spirit
SPIRIT 4 - a lesser spirit

MARLEY - Scrooge's ghastly partner, who begins the haunt
THE PAST - the first Ghost, a delicate being of light and memory
THE PRESENT - the second Ghost, a giant—full-voiced and robed.
YET TO COME - the third Ghost, a phantom cloaked in black

SCROOGE - A grumpy old miser who has an eventful night
BOY - an image of Scrooge's boyhood self
YOUNG EBENEZER - Scrooge as a young boy at school
TEEN EBENEZER - Scrooge as a school youth
EBENEZER - Scrooge as a young man

BOB CRATCHIT - Scrooge's apprentice, underpaid and misused
MRS. CRATCHIT - A beleaguered woman
PETER - Bob Cratchit's eldest son, a young man
BELINDA - Bob Cratchit's youngest daughter, a girl
MARTHA - Bob Cratchit's eldest child, a young factory worker
TINY TIM - Bob Cratchit's youngest child, a sickly, crippled boy

FRED - Scrooge's nephew by his long-dead sister
CLARA - Fred's wife, a woman of similar age to Fred

MR. MCCAWBER - a man in debt and on the verge of debtor's prison
MRS. MCCAWBER - a woman of questionable adorations

POSTMAN - a diligent deliverer of letters

FATHER - Scrooge's father
YOUNG FAN - Scrooge's sister as a young girl
FAN - Scrooge's beloved sister, a young woman
JAMES - a friend of Ebenezer's at school

BELLE - Scrooge's fiancé, a young woman
FEZZIWIG - a fatherly old fellow, Scrooge's employer
MRS. FEZZIWIG - a lively woman
DICK - Scrooge's co-worker, a young man

MINER 1 - one of three sooty ore miners
MINER 2
MINER 3
WATCHMAN 1 - one of a pair of salty old lighthouse keepers
WATCHMAN 2
COLLECTOR 1 - a fundraiser for charity
COLLECTOR 2
FRIEND 1 - one of two friends of Fred
FRIEND 2

THE BOY (IGNORANCE) - a dirty, miserable child
THE GIRL (WANT) - a dirty miserable child

LONDONER 1 - one of four English commoners
LONDONER 2
LONDONER 3
LONDONER 4

THIEF - one of a pair of wretched thieves
MRS. DILBER - a thief (and a housekeeper)
OLD JOE - a pawnbroker

DOCTOR - a physician who tends Tiny Tim
URCHIN - a boy on the street
BEGGAR - a wretch
TURKEY MAN - a man beset with a gargantuan bird
SYDNEY - a spirit judged favorably
URIAH - an 'umble spirit judged harshly

ACT I

ACT I

SCENE 1

Darkness. A COMPANY *of lesser spirits hover over the face of the void, all silently undulating upon the formless stage.*

SPIRIT 1 (LEAD) *enters burdened by an enormous tome. The* SPIRIT *sits behind a high desk and flops open the book.*

SPIRIT 1 (LEAD): Are we ready?

The COMPANY *of spirits murmur assent in harsh whispers.*

SPIRIT 1 (LEAD): Very well. Bring them.

A group of forlorn spirts step forward.

SPIRIT 1 (LEAD): Name?

URIAH: (*obsequiously*) We are very 'umble, Spirit, and it's my pleasure to offer my name. A most 'umble name it is . . . Uriah He—

SPIRIT 1 (LEAD): Ugh! Just give him an ample iron and get on with it.

THE COMPANY: Bind him.

URIAH: But we are so very 'umble, sir . . .

SPIRIT 1 (LEAD): Next.

URIAH *is dragged away roughly. Another spirit steps forward.*

SPIRIT 1 (LEAD): Name?

SYDNEY: Sir?

SPIRIT 1 (LEAD): Your name.

SYDNEY: My apologies, Spirit. Lost my head there for a moment. Sydney, I was . . . I think . . . Carton.

SPIRIT 1 (LEAD): (*checking his book*): Another lawyer. That's unfortunate, but . . . hmmm . . . what's this? Oh. That's a thing finely done. Well done indeed. It's a pleasure to meet you, sir. I think you'll go to some far better rest down the hall . . . Just there.

SYDNEY *is gently escorted offstage.*

SPIRIT 1 (LEAD): Don't see many like that do we? Next.

MARLEY'*s ghost approaches.* SPIRIT 1 (LEAD) *checks his book.*

SPIRIT 1 (LEAD): Well? Name?

MARLEY: Jacob Marley.

SPIRIT 1 (LEAD): A banker, a counter of coin . . . usury . . . corruption . . . greed . . . the usual.

SPIRIT 1 (LEAD) *scribbles in his book and then looks up expectantly.*

THE COMPANY: Bind him.

The company of spirits bind MARLEY *with chains.*

MARLEY: Wait!

MARLEY *breaks away from his captors and pleads at the desk.*

SPIRIT 1 (LEAD): What's this?

MARLEY: Bind me in my rightful chain, but allow me to intercede for another.

SPIRIT 4:   What other?

SPIRIT 3:   Speak.

MARLEY: I give you a knot to unravel.

MARLEY *steps up to the desk and puts his finger upon another name in the book.*

SPIRIT 2:   Some new mystery?

SPIRIT 1 (LEAD): No. An old one, I think.

MARLEY: Out of what is old, something new may yet be wrought.

SPIRIT 1 (LEAD): To shape something new . . .

SPIRIT 2:   Something old . . .

SPIRIT 3:   Must die.

A beat.

SPIRIT 1 (LEAD): If you choose this now, your torment may cross ages upon ages.

MARLEY: (*beat*) So be it.

SPIRIT 1 (LEAD): Double his iron.

A group of phantoms emerge from the shadows. They surround MARLEY *and bind him in further chains. He is burdened to the ground under their weight, scarcely able to move.*

SPIRIT 4:   Where then do we begin?

SPIRIT 3:   With the present?

SPIRIT 4:   Or will it be the future?

MARLEY: No. Go back.

SPIRIT 1 (LEAD): The past, then?

MARLEY: Yes. Yes! The boy.

THE COMPANY: (*whispered*) The boy!

The silhouette of THE BOY *appears in ghastly light.*

THE BOY: (*Gesture: arm extended, palm up*)

SPIRIT 4:   Yes. There is, perhaps, a chance.

SPIRIT 3:   A chance so faint that it may flicker out . . .

SPIRIT 2:   . . . like the spent wick of an old candle.

One of the onlooking spirits blows on the child and he fades away.

SPIRIT 1 (LEAD): How, then, shall we proceed? From the begin-
                ning?

SPIRIT 4:   But which beginning?

SPIRIT 2:   There are so many!

SPIRIT 1 (LEAD): We shall begin with an ending. For every ending
                gives birth a new story.

SPIRIT 2:   A begending?

SPIRIT 4:   I don't understand.

SPIRIT 2:   If it all goes sour, don't say I didn't tell you so.

SPIRIT 1 (LEAD): It is time. Are you ready?

MARLEY: I'm ready.

ALL: (*whispered*) Show us the beginning!

A great bell sounds the stroke of the hour.

SPIRIT 1 (LEAD): To begin with . . .

SPIRIT 3:   Marley . . .

A door opens centerstage, and in the doorway is an upright coffin shrouded in light.

SPIRIT 4:   . . . was . . .

The coffin lid swings open and the chains drag MARLEY *into its throat.*

SPIRIT 1 (LEAD): . . . DEAD!

The coffin lid is snapped shut with a thud.

SPIRIT 2:   (*checking the security of the lid*) Dead?

SPIRIT 4:   Mostly dead?

SPIRIT 1 (LEAD): Entirely dead. There is no doubt whatsoever about THAT.

The lights reveal a London street.

SPIRIT 1 (LEAD): The register of his burial was signed by . . .

As each of the following speak, they step to the coffin and sign a paper. As the scene takes shape, the spirits take on the parts and appearances of Londoners.

SPIRIT 1 (LEAD): The clergyman.

SPIRIT 2:   The clerk.

SPIRIT 3:   The undertaker.

SPIRIT 4:   (*opening the coffin to look*) But are we *sure* he was . . .

SPIRIT 1 (LEAD): Even HE signed!

SPIRIT 4:   Who?

SPIRIT 2:   So *he* knew he was . . .

SPIRIT 1 (LEAD): Of course *he* did. They were partners for years.

SPIRIT 4:   Who was?

SPIRIT 1 (LEAD): *He* was his sole executor . . .

SPIRIT 2:   . . . his sole assign . . .

SPIRIT 1 (LEAD): . . . his sole friend and mourner.

SPIRIT 4:   So then Jacob Marley really was . . .

The door upstage flies open and a stark figure emerges silhouetted in light.

SCROOGE: DEAD as a doornail!

The company of spirits all gasp and shrink away.

The spirits whisper to one another in exclamations: "It's Scrooge!" "Ebenezer Scrooge!" "It's HIM!"

SCROOGE *stalks downstage. He extends his arm* GESTURING *with palm out as if to push away the coffin as it's drawn through the door and vanishes.*

The company give him a wide berth as he strolls across the stage on his cane. He's shadowed at a distance by the BOY, *who mimics many of* SCROOGE'S *mannerisms.* SCROOGE *ignores the* BOY.

SPIRIT 1 (LEAD): And old Ebenezer Scrooge never did paint out Jacob's name. There it stood for seven years above the counting house door.

ALL: Scrooge & Marley.

SPIRIT 2: Look at him! He's secret . . .

SPIRIT 1 (LEAD): . . . and solitary as an oyster.

SPIRIT 3: No beggars implore him to bestow an alm.

SPIRIT 1 (LEAD): No children ever ask him for a candy or a crumb.

SPIRIT 4: Why not?

SPIRIT 1 (LEAD): It's all the very thing he likes.

SPIRIT 2: To edge his way along the path of life . . .

SPIRIT 3: . . . warning all human sympathy to keep its distance.

SPIRIT 1 (LEAD): And listen! Here comes his shrewd old croak!

SPIRIT 3: Merry Christmas, sir!

SCROOGE: *(looking around and leveling his cane at the company in turn)* Bah! HUM . . . bug!

SPIRIT 4: Is it today?

SPIRIT 1 (LEAD): Not today.

SPIRIT 4:   It's tomorrow isn't it? Tomorrow is . . .

ALL: Christmas!

SCROOGE: You there. Clear out from that door, and find
                 some other stoop to haunt.

SPIRIT 4:   Merry Christmas, sir.

SPIRIT 1 (LEAD): And here we are. Christmas Eve. A beginning.

The COMPANY *exits.*

SCENE 2

SCROOGE *glowers and then enters the office as the* BOY *watches and is the last of the* COMPANY *to leave.* BOB *is at work in a corner, shivering.*

BOB: Good morning, sir.

SCROOGE: Morning it is, but it's quality is yet in question.

BOB: (*handing* SCROOGE *a stack of papers*) I've nearly completed yesterday's books, sir. Mr. McCawber says he will be by later to pay up his interest.

SCROOGE: If he doesn't it'll go poorly with him tomorrow.

BOB: I suppose so, sir.

SCROOGE: Was there something else?

BOB: Oh, well, sir . . . I thought I might ask . . .

SCROOGE *rounds an evil eye upon* BOB, *and* BOB *shrinks and quiets.*

SCROOGE: Ask what?

BOB: Yes, well, about that . . .

FRED *bursts in through the door, interrupting.*

FRED: Merry Christmas, uncle! God save you!

SCROOGE: (*startled*) Ahh! Humbug!

BOB: Hello, Fred!

FRED: Christmas a humbug, uncle? You don't mean that!

SCROOGE: I do mean it! What right have you to be merry? What reason have you to be merry? You're poor enough.

FRED: What right have you to be dismal? What reason have you to be so morose? You're rich enough.

SCROOGE: I have no time for your nonsense. Whatever you want you won't find it here.

FRED: Don't be cross, uncle.

SCROOGE: What else can I be when I live in such a world of fools?

FRED: Am I a fool?

SCROOGE: What's Christmas to you but a time for paying bills without money. A time for finding yourself a year older, but not an hour richer.

FRED: Come now. Surely you can't think . . .

SCROOGE: If I could work my will, every idiot who goes about with "Merry Christmas" on his lips would be boiled with his own pudding and buried with a stake of holly through his heart.

FRED: Uncle!

SCROOGE: Don't "uncle" me. Keep Christmas in your own
                 way and leave me to keep it in mine.

FRED: But you don't keep it.

SCROOGE: Let me leave it alone then. Much good has it ever
                 done me!

FRED: Much good? I've always thought of Christmas-
                 time as a good time—even apart from its sacred
                 origin, which is much good in itself.

SCROOGE: Much good has it ever done you!

FRED: In fact, it's the only time I know of when men
                 and women seem to open their shut-up hearts
                 and think of people below them as fellow passen-
                 gers to the grave—rather than some other race of
                 creature altogether.

SCROOGE: Miserable creatures every one.

FRED: And therefore, uncle, though it has never put a
                 scrap of gold in my pocket, I believe it has done
                 me good, and will do me good, and so I say, God
                 bless it!

BOB *leaps from his stool and applauds involuntarily.* SCROOGE
rounds on him with an evil eye that silences him mid-clap.

SCROOGE: Another sound from you, and you'll keep your
                 Christmas by losing your situation!

                 (SCROOGE *rounds back on* FRED *with a devious
                 smile.*)

                 Well, well, well, Fred. Nephew. You are quite a

	powerful speaker, sir. It is a wonder you don't go into Parliament.
FRED:	Don't be angry, uncle. Come and dine with us tomorrow.
SCROOGE:	Dine with you? Pah! I should rather see you in h—
FRED:	But why? Why, uncle?
SCROOGE:	Why? "Why" has never got anyone anywhere or any good. Don't bother me with your idle "why." Why does the floor creak? Why does the kettle whistle? Why did you get married?
FRED:	Because I fell in love.
SCROOGE:	(*mockingly*) In love. Hah. Now there's the only thing more ridiculous than a merry Christmas. Good afternoon!
FRED:	I am sorry to find you so resolute. But I have attempted peace and I'll keep my humor to the last. So a Merry Christmas, uncle!
SCROOGE:	Good afternoon!
FRED:	And a happy New Year!
SCROOGE:	Good afternoon!
FRED:	(*to* BOB) And the same to you, Mr. Cratchit.
BOB:	I thank you, sir.

BOB *opens the door to show* FRED *out.* SCROOGE *pauses and removes a locket from his pocket. He rubs it thoughtfully for a moment before*

COLLECTOR 1 *and* COLLECTOR 2 *enter. He quickly secrets the locket away.*

COLLECTOR 1: (*referring to a list of businesses*) This is, ah . . . Scrooge & Marley's!

COLLECTOR 2: Have I the pleasure of addressing Mr. Scrooge or Mr. Marley?

SCROOGE: Jacob Marley is dead seven years this night. What do you want?

COLLECTOR 1: I am sorry to hear of Mr. Marley's decease, but we have no doubt his generosity is well represented by his surviving partner. Perhaps in honor of the mournful anniversary of his passage?

SCROOGE's *eyebrows crawl up his forehead in disbelief.*

COLLECTOR 2: (*holding out a journal and withdrawing his pen*) In this season of the year, Mr. Scrooge, it is more than usually desirable that we should make some provision for the poor and destitute who suffer greatly.

COLLECTOR 1: As I'm sure you are aware.

COLLECTOR 2: Thousands are in want of common necessities.

SCROOGE: Are they now?

COLLECTOR 1: Hundreds of thousands are in want of common comfort, sir.

SCROOGE: I see, but are there no prisons?

COLLECTOR 1: Prisons? Yes, there are plenty of prisons.

SCROOGE: And the union workhouses? Are they still in operation?

COLLECTOR 1:   They are. Still.

COLLECTOR 2:   Though I wish we could say they were not.

SCROOGE: Oh! Wonderful. I was afraid that something had occurred to stop them in their useful course. I'm very glad to hear it.

COLLECTOR 2:   (*glancing nervously at* COLLECTOR 1) A few of us are raising a fund to buy the poor some meat and drink and means of warmth. We choose this time, Christmastime, because it is a time, of all others, when Want is keenly felt, and Abundance rejoices. What shall I put you down for?

SCROOGE: Nothing.

COLLECTOR 2:   Ah hah. You wish to be anonymous. Very respectable.

SCROOGE: I wish to be left alone!

                (SCROOGE GESTURES *with his arm as if to push them away*)

                I don't make merry myself at Christmas and I certainly can't afford to make idle people merry.

COLLECTOR 1:   Idle people?

SCROOGE: I support the establishments I have mentioned, and they cost quite enough. Let those who are badly off go there.

COLLECTOR 2:   Many cannot go there.

COLLECTOR 1:   And many would rather die.

SCROOGE: If they would rather die, then they had better do it and decrease the surplus population.

COLLECTOR 1 *and* COLLECTOR 2 *are flabbergasted.*

SCROOGE: Now, then, Good afternoon!

SCROOGE *shoves them out the door, closes it, and turns to approach his desk with self-satisfied pride.*

SCROOGE: Haven't you something more profitable to look at?

BOB: Yes, sir. But, ah, sir . . . I wonder if I might have a word about—

The door opens and MR. MCCAWBER *enters in high spirits. Followed by an obsequious* MRS. MCCAWBER.

MR. MCCAWBER: Mr. Scrooge! There you are. A Merry Christmas, my good fellow. What a fine day it is, don't you think so?

MRS. MCCAWBER: As fine a day as we've ever seen, it is.

BOB: Good day, Mr. McCawber. Mrs. McCawber.

SCROOGE: My day is worse by the minute and I little expect your appearance will better it.

MR. MCCAWBER: Oh, but I shall better it, my good man.

MRS. MCCAWBER: He shall! Just you watch him? I've known him to better nearly everything I ever saw!

MR. MCCAWBER: I have come for that precise and desirable effect,

and you shall soon dwell in the sure knowledge
that I, Wilkins McCawber, have presented upon
this day creditable assurances of great deeds and
a boon of long hoped-for remuneration.

MRS. MCCAWBER: Looooong hoped for!

SCROOGE: Get to the point, McCawber.

MR. MCCAWBER: Yes, sir. Without even the shortest delay!

MRS. MCCAWBER: He never does delay. Do you, dear?

SCROOGE: If you're late again, you'll eat your Christmas
                dinner with the indigent population at
                Marshalsea prison.

MRS. MCCAWBER *quakes and squeals in fright.*

MR. MCCAWBER: (*with great pomp*) Yes, sir. About that, sir. I
                am sure you are in no way unprepared to obtain
                what I have brought you and, well, in short, sir,
                in the very shortest terms, it is my pleasure to
                leave it with you.

MRS. MCCAWBER: Yes, leave it with him, Mr. McCawber.

MR. MCCAWBER: In fact I could not leave this office without
                acquitting myself of the pecuniary part of my
                obligation to you and your very sensible terms.
                In fact, and in short, it would weigh upon my
                mind to an insupportable extent if I did not do
                so with the utmost alacrity.

MR. MCCAWBER *removes an envelope from his coat with great
flourish.*

MRS. MCCAWBER: *Such* alacrity! The best I've ever known!

MR. McCAWBER: I now hold in my hand, an envelope, which accomplishes the desired object, and I am happy to maintain my moral dignity, and to know that I can once more walk erect before my fellow man and will not live under the threat of a debtor's prison on Christmas Day. Good Mr. Scrooge, I thank you.

MR. McCAWBER *extends the envelope to* SCROOGE *who takes it suspiciously.*

MR. McCAWBER: A Merry Christmas to you, sir!

MRS. McCAWBER: Come along dear, show me your alacrity!

MRS. McCAWBER *quickly and nervously drags* MR. McCAWBER *through the door and they exit as* SCROOGE *snarls and opens the envelope.*

SCROOGE: Villain!

BOB: Don't be cruel, sir.

SCROOGE: An I. O. U.! Curse the day I lent a thruppence to anyone that goes by the name McCawber. He'll see the inside of Marshalsea prison or I'm not Ebenezer Scrooge.

BOB: But his children, sir. Is there nothing that can be done? After all it's Chr—

SCROOGE: Keep to your ledger book, Bob Cratchit. I pay for your work, not your questions.

SCROOGE *and* BOB *set about their work.*

SPIRIT 4:   Is he always like that?

Spirit 1 (Lead): Always. Watch this.

> (*begins to sing a carol*)
>
> We wish you a Merry Christmas . . .

Bob *rushes to the window to listen.* Scrooge *wads up two balls of paper and stuffs them into his ears.*

Spirit 4:   I feel badly for him.

Spirit 1 (Lead): He has no idea what's coming.

Spirit 4:   (*the church bell rings*) Is that that the bell? Is it happening?

Spirit 1 (Lead): Not yet. Keep quiet.

The Boy *looks in at the window, unseen.* Bob *cleans his desk and packs his satchel.* Mrs. Cratchit *quietly peeks in at the door and waves at* Bob. *He smiles at her nervously and then meekly approaches* Scrooge*'s desk.*

Bob: . . . s . . . sir . . . I, ahem, earlier, I meant to ask . . .

Scrooge: You'll want all day tomorrow, I suppose?

Bob: If quite convenient, sir.

Scrooge: Well it's not convenient. If I was to dock you half-a-crown for it, you'd think yourself ill-used. Isn't that right?

Bob *fumbles for an answer.*

Scrooge: And yet, you don't think me ill-used, when I pay a day's wages for no work, do you?

Bob: I . . . I think it's but once a year, sir.

SCROOGE: A poor excuse for picking a man's pocket every twenty-fifth of December.

MRS. CRATCHIT *enters boldly and strides to the desk.* SCROOGE *looks on with amazement.*

BOB: My dear, please, let me . . .

MRS. CRATCHIT: Sir, he . . . *we* . . . had hoped to take the day to visit a physician with our son.

BOB: He's been poorly this year, sir. The cold, you see, it's in his bones, sir.

MRS. CRATCHIT: I tell him how strong he is and he believes me and tries to make it true, but to see him, sir.

BOB: He's not as a boy should be, sir, its in his bones, I think, and well, it goes hard on his mother, and on me too . . . sir.

SCROOGE: I suppose you must have the whole day or there will never be an end of this maudlin display.

BOB *shrugs apologetically.*

SCROOGE: See you're here all the earlier next morning.

MRS. CRATCHIT: Thank you, sir! Merry Chr—

BOB: (*cutting her off*) Early as early can be. The sun himself won't be earlier. Thank you, sir. And Merr—

MRS. CRATCHIT: Merry Christmas!

SCROOGE *levels an evil grimace, and* BOB *and* MRS. CRATCHIT *hustle out.* SCROOGE, *muttering to himself, locks up shop, and walks home. He's followed at a distance by the* BOY.

SCROOGE *turns and the* BOY *catches his eye. The* BOY GESTURES, *reaching out to palm up.* SCROOGE GESTURES *back, extending his arm to the child, palm out, as if to keep him at bay.*

SCENE 3

The wind howls. Passersby flit about, quieting as they pass SCROOGE.

SPIRIT 4: He creeps along the street like an unwanted odor.

SPIRIT 1 (LEAD): He's proud of his misery, like an old soldier with a bitter wound from a ill-remembered war.

SPIRIT 2: The nearest thing he knows to joy is the prick of pride upon wounding another.

SPIRIT 1 (LEAD): And so he drives his path through London, filling the world with scars like his own.

Sounds of laughter erupt as light illumines a silhouette of a happy family. SCROOGE *scowls at it and hurries past.*

A carol begins and another light illumines a silhouette of people singing together.

A BEGGAR *approaches* SCROOGE *with palm out, but* SCROOGE *mutters and grimaces and hobbles past.*

SCROOGE *stops and turns. The* BOY *stares at* SCROOGE *in silence.*

SCROOGE: What do you want? Leave me be.

The BOY *ignores* SCROOGE'S *pleas. He stares quietly as* SCROOGE *GESTURES, extending his hand toward the boy again, as if to say "keep away," then mounts his doorstep.*

SCROOGE *fumbles for his key. A group of people rush past and* SCROOGE *looks nervously at the strange, silent* BOY, *who backs quietly into the shadows.*

SCROOGE: Leave me be and begone.

SCROOGE *turns to the door and* MARLEY'S *face is staring at him where the knocker should be.*

MARLEY: (*whispering*) Scrooooooooge.

SCROOGE *startles and looks around. When* SCROOGE *looks back again, the knocker is a knocker. He knocks to be sure.*

SCROOGE: (*muttering*) Hmmph. Dead as a doornail.

SCROOGE *enters the house, lights his candle and looks around timidly. He checks and double checks the knocker. Then closes, locks, and double locks, the door.*

MRS. DILBER: Is somethin' the matter, sir?

SCROOGE *jumps in fright.*

SCROOGE: What? The matter? No, nothing.

MRS. DILBER: The linens is washed, and the drapes and all the bedclothes is fresh, sir. Is there anything else?

SCROOGE: Have you mended that shirt of mine. I can't suffer a garment with a hole, Mrs. Dilber. If I've said it once I've said it a dozen times.

MRS. DILBER: Yes, sir. Patched good as new, it is. Good as Sunday morning, if I don't say so myself. If there's nothing else, then I shall see you in three days. Got me kinfolk come for Christmas see?

MRS. DILBER, *pushes past* SCROOGE *and unlocks the door as she speaks.*

SCROOGE: Have you seen a boy about?

MRS. DILBER: A boy? No sir, I never did. I don't put up with boys under no circumstances and they don't put up with me neither.

SCROOGE: Very well. Goodnight, Mrs. Dilber.

MRS. DILBER: Goodnight yourself. And a merry—

SCROOGE *pushes her out the door and closes it.*

SCROOGE: Good night and good riddance.

SCROOGE *turns to the darkened house and lifts his candle. Then he turns and locks and double-locks the door. The* COMPANY *of spirits enter and swirl.*

SPIRIT 1 (LEAD): The house is full of creaks.

SPIRIT 4:   What was that?!

SPIRIT 1 (LEAD): Every room has an echo.

SPIRIT 2:   And every cellar . . .

SPIRIT 3:   . . . every nook . . .

SPIRIT 1 (LEAD): . . . every cranny sends up a peal of disquieting rattles as he stalks the desolate hall.

SPIRIT 4:   But for the lonely candle all the house crouches in darkness.

SPIRIT 1 (LEAD): Darkness is cheap. Scrooge likes it.

SPIRIT 2:   I don't like it.

SCROOGE: What's that? Is anyone there?

SCROOGE *timidly walks to his chamber, checking under tables and behind doors to verify his solitude.*

SPIRIT 4:   No one under the table?

SPIRIT 1 (LEAD): No one behind the door.

SPIRIT 3:   Not a soul beneath the sofa.

SPIRIT 2:   No one at all behind the fireplace grate.

All stop and listen, including SCROOGE.

SPIRIT 4:   Did you hear that?

SPIRIT 1 (LEAD): Quiet. They're coming.

SPIRIT 2:   I still don't think it's going to work.

SPIRIT 1 (LEAD): Hush!

The company of spirits fade into the shadows.

SCROOGE: Hmmph.

SCROOGE *lights a meager fire and undresses to his bedclothes. He sits and begins to eat a hard knob of bread as he studies a book of accounts.*

SPIRIT 4:   What's he doing?

SPIRIT 2:   Is he counting in his books?

SPIRIT 1 (LEAD): Watch this.

SPIRIT 1 (LEAD) *steps to the bell upon the wall and lightly rings it.* SCROOGE *freezes. He stares at it. The bell goes silent.*

SPIRIT 4:   You'll spoil it!

SPIRIT 2:   Are they coming yet?

SPIRIT 4:   No. Wait!

SPIRIT 1 (LEAD): Trust me.

SCROOGE *begins to gnaw his bread again and* SPIRIT 1 (LEAD) *rings the bell once more, louder this time. Again,* SCROOGE *stares it into silence and returns to his gnawing.*

He eyes the bell. It keeps quiet.

He eyes it again. Quiet.

He bows his head back to his book and the bell is rung once more. SCROOGE *leaps to his feet and seizes the bell.*

SCROOGE: Quiet! Quiet! You'll ring when you're rung or never at all.

SCROOGE *returns to his chair, but as soon as he sits. The* COMPANY *all begin to ring bells in such a cacophony that they threaten to shake down the house.* SCROOGE *gathers himself and rips a bell from the wall. He throws it on the floor. He smothers it with a pillow. Silence.*

SCROOGE: Humbug. Do you hear that? HumBUG!

He slowly backs away from the "dead" bell in suspicion.

The COMPANY *look around and gasp. They whisper to one another.*

"It's time." "Look out!" "He's here!"

Scrooge *begins to sit and BOOM. A great knock shakes the door.*
Scrooge *hides behind his chair.*

Scrooge: No. No, sir. I don't believe it. Humbug it all. No
ringing. No knocking. No strange little boy in
the night, I say. Humbug it.

BOOM!

Scrooge: No.

BOOM!

Scrooge;   Not one bit.

The clatter of great chains on the stair.

CLATTER. BOOM!

Scrooge: Oh, definitely not.

CLATTER. BOOM!

Silence. Silence. Scrooge *timid peeks out and...*

The door flies open with a crash and Marley *enters shrouded in
spectral light, bound all about in chains that reach out the door and
tether him to unknown anchors beyond.*

Marley: *Scrooge!*

Scrooge: You aren't there. You aren't real!

Scrooge Gestures, *hand out to push the spectre away, but is inef-
fective.* Marley *is inexorable.*

Marley: *Ebenezer Scrooge!*

SCROOGE: Burgle me and begone! Leave me in peace!

MARLEY: Look at me. Ask me who I was.

SCROOGE: I don't care who you are or who you were.

MARLEY: In life, I was your partner.

A beat.

SCROOGE: (*peeking up curiously*) Jacob?

MARLEY: You know me, Ebenezer.

SCROOGE: Jacob Marley? But you're dead. I saw you.

ALL: (*whispered*) Dead as a doornail.

MARLEY: Seven looong years dead.

SCROOGE *creeps carefully out from behind his chair and examines* MARLEY.

SCROOGE: Jacob? You can't be.

MARLEY: Doubt will serve you ill tonight, old friend.

SCROOGE: Yes. Well. If you are him, you look ... remarkably
                ... ambulant for a man of his desiccated condi-
                tion.

The chains tug at MARLEY, *he tugs back.*

A beat.

MARLEY: You don't believe in me, do you, Ebenezer.

SCROOGE: Why should I? You may be an undigested bit of
                beef, a crumb of cheese, a fragment of an under-
                done potato.

MARLEY: Am I now? A morsel of mortality? See you nothing more? Nothing grave?

MARLEY *and* SCROOGE *consider one another in silence.*

SCROOGE: Humbug, I tell you. Hum—

MARLEY *raises a terrific groan and shakes his chains.* SCROOGE *screams and cowers behind his chair.*

SCROOGE: Have mercy. Have mercy, Jacob. Why do you trouble me?

MARLEY: Do you believe in me or not?

SCROOGE: I do! I swear it.

MARLEY: Remember that oath for upon it is tethered your sole salvation.

SCROOGE: Talk sensibly. What have I done to attract the traffic of spirits?

MARLEY: I am doomed to wander the world and witness what I cannot share but might have shared on earth. Do you hear me? The goodwill I withheld in life now holds me to my doom in death.

SCROOGE: Yes. I can see you are...inconveniently...fettered. I suppose you want me to ask you who has done this to you? And why?

MARLEY: I wear the chain I forged in life. Link by link, I made it. Yard by yard, I girded it on of my own free will, and of my own free will I wore it. Is its pattern strange to you? Do you not know its shape and the manner of its making?

SCROOGE *shakes his head and turns away.*

SCROOGE: I don't know what you mean.

MARLEY: Yours was full as heavy and as long as mine seven
                Christmas Eves ago, and you have labored greatly
                on it since.

SCROOGE: No. This is all some fantasy of the brain. You
                aren't real. Go away. Hum—

The COMPANY *of spirits bring forth spectral chains and slowly move
toward* SCROOGE *with them.* SCROOGE *sees this and cowers.*

MARLEY: I see it wound about you even now. Can you not
                feel it tighten about your immortal soul? Yours is
                a ponderous chain!

SCROOGE: Get away!

The COMPANY *backs away with the chains but hover nearby.*

SCROOGE: Why do you talk this way, Jacob? Can you not
                speak some comfort to me?

MARLEY: Little time is all I am permitted. I have been
                seven endless years in coming to you tonight,
                and the little time I have is ending.

SCROOGE: In seven years you've journeyed but this far?
                I make the walk in but a quarter of the clock.
                You've got even slower than you were in life.

MARLEY: Captive, bound, and double-ironed! Not to
                know that no space of regret can make amends
                for one's life misused . . .

SCROOGE: What are you saying, Jacob? I don't understand.

MARLEY: . . . not to know the ceaseless labors of immortal creatures—for this earth must pass into eternity before the good toward which it's bent is all achieved. Yet such an ignorant beast was I! Look on my torment!

SCROOGE: But you were always a good man of business, Jacob!

MARLEY: Humankind was my business. Charity, mercy, forbearance, and benevolence were all my business. The dealings of my trade were but a drop of water in the vast ocean of my business!

SCROOGE: Don't be hard upon me, Jacob.

MARLEY: Then attend me closely, Ebenezer. You have yet hope of escaping my fate. A chance of my procuring. My gift to you at great cost.

The chains tug violently at MARLEY. *He resists.*

SCROOGE: A gift?

MARLEY: You will be haunted by three Spirits.

SCROOGE: Spirits? Is that the gift?

MARLEY: It is.

SCROOGE: That you have procured? For me?

MARLEY: It is.

SCROOGE: I . . . I think I'd rather not.

MARLEY: Expect the first when the bell tolls One.

SCROOGE: Couldn't I take them all at once and have it over with?

MARLEY: Expect the second on the stroke of Two. The
            third shall come when the last stroke of Three
            has ceased to toll.

SCROOGE: But I need my sleep, Jacob!

MARLEY: Look to see me no more, Ebenezer, and look
            that, for your own sake, you remember what has
            passed between us here!

MARLEY *stands and the chains tighten around him. He reaches out
to* SCROOGE *but the chains jerk him backward.* MARLEY *struggles
but the chains drag him through the door with a mounting wailing
from beyond as if he is being withdrawn into some great torment
unseen.*

SCROOGE *follows him until* MARLEY *vanishes into the ghastly light
beyond the door.* SCROOGE *looks out and recoils in horror as the
wailing crescendos and then is suddenly silenced by the slamming of
the door.* SCROOGE *locks and double-locks it securely.*

SCROOGE: (*unconvincingly*) . . . humbug . . .

SCROOGE *retreats to his bed, crawls into it and pulls the sheets up to
his eyes, looking out for one brief moment and seeing the clock poised
upon the brink of ONE, then he pulls the sheet up over his head in
silence.*

SCENE 4

Tick. Tock. Tick. Tock. Tick. Tock.

SPIRIT 3:   She's almost here.

SPIRIT 1 (LEAD): Quiet.

SPIRIT 4:   Do you feel that? She's close!

The toll of ONE.

DONG.

SPIRIT 1 (LEAD): And so begins the long, dark night of Ebenezer
                Scrooge.

The Spirits exit. SCROOGE *lowers the sheets and looks out.*

Silence.

SCROOGE: Hah. The hour itself. And nothing else.

From the mirror, a faint light appears and begins to grow. SCROOGE
*whimpers. The glow grows into a small figure with a crown of light
and a torch in one hand and a large cap in the other. It glides out
of the mirror and up to* SCROOGE's *bedside and stares at him in*

silence.

SCROOGE: Are you the Spirit whose coming was foretold?

THE PAST: I am!

SCROOGE: Hmmph. You aren't half so dreadful as your kind is generally described.

THE PAST: Hmm. And in what manner do you imagine I am described?

SCROOGE: I only meant that . . .

THE PAST: I know very well what you meant, and many other things beside. Some spirits, it's true, may administer dread and terror to humankind. While others offer delight or foretelling. And others still are mysteries yet-hidden until their time is full prepared.

SCROOGE: Then tell me, what manner of spirit are you?

THE PAST: There are none other of my kind like me, Ebenezer Scrooge. I am the Ghost of Christmas Past.

SCROOGE: Past?

THE PAST: Your past.

SCROOGE: Hmm. I see.

                Would you mind putting on your cap. Your light disquiets me.

THE PAST: You would so quickly snuff out the light I offer. It was you and those like you who made this cap. You who wish the world a darker place than it

was made to be. But listen to me now: this illu-
mination is a gift. Will you refuse it as you have
so many times before?

SCROOGE: I swear that I have never set my hand to the fash-
ioning of hats. That is not my business.

THE PAST: Hmm. Is it not?

SCROOGE: No. And what is your business here?

THE PAST: I'm am here to . . . to draw out, to bind up, to dig
in, to excavate and investigate . . . to dissect and
conciliate!

SCROOGE: Did you say "dissect?"

THE PAST: My business, Ebenezer Scrooge, is your welfare.

SCROOGE: My welfare? Well I suggest my welfare is best
served by a night's sleep. So if you'll put on your
cap and quiet your light, I'll . . .

THE PAST: Rise! And walk with me!

SCROOGE: (*moaning*) Oh. No please.

SCROOGE GESTURES *to push the spirit away.* THE PAST *takes*
SCROOGE'*s hand and pulls him from his bed.*

THE PAST: Come with me!

SCROOGE: Where? Where are you taking me?

THE PAST: Backward. Forward. Inward. Outward. The past
is as long and dim as memory itself, and all its
roads are open to me. Do you not hear it?

SCROOGE: Hear it? Hear what?

THE PAST: The strains of Memory. It whimpers and groans, for you have hidden it away and it longs to be set free. Come with me, Ebenezer Scrooge, let us be explorers a while along the misty roads of remembrance.

SCROOGE: I am too old for explorations.

THE PAST: Come!

SCROOGE *is compelled by the command.* THE PAST *leads him to the window and steps out into the air.* SCROOGE *stops upon the sill.*

SCROOGE: No. Please! I cannot. I am mortal and will fall.

THE PAST: You are in my keep tonight, Ebenezer Scrooge. Bear but a touch of my hand. Here.

THE PAST *lays its hand upon* SCROOGE*'s heart.*

THE PAST: And you will be upheld in more than you can know.

SCROOGE *takes a breath and then steps out into the air. He is upheld, and he laughs.*

SCENE 5

THE PAST *leads* SCROOGE *across the stage as the scene changes from the cool muted tones of a London night, to the bright shades of crisp day.*

SCROOGE: Good heaven. I know this place.

THE PAST: Name it. Call it to life.

SCROOGE: I was a boy here.

YOUNG EBENEZER/THE BOY *enters.* SCROOGE *recoils and puts out his hand.*

SCROOGE: Get away!

The Boy doffs his cap to SCROOGE *and runs past.*

SCROOGE: I've seen him before.

THE PAST: Have you?

SCROOGE: He follows me—watches me. A strange, sad child. What is he doing here? Where are we going?

THE PAST: You know the way. Do you not?

SCROOGE *pauses in thought a moment, looking around as memory draws a scene to life in his mind.*

SCROOGE: I remember as if it were yesterday. I could walk it blindfolded.

THE PAST: And yet you have forgotten for so many years. I wonder why? Lead on. Show me.

SCROOGE *and* THE PAST *walk.* SCROOGE *excitedly remembering things along the way.*

SCROOGE: I remember a tree. I climbed it every summer? It must be here . . . or there! And I recall a gate. It led up to the cart-driver's house. What was his name?

THE PAST: Barkis?

SCROOGE: Yes, good old Mr. Barkis! And the town must be near.

THE PAST: That way, I think.

SCROOGE: I can nearly see it . . .

The COMPANY *run past, calling to one another.*

SPIRIT 3:   Hurry up, Oliver!

SPIRIT 4:   Where are we going?

SPIRIT 2:   Slow down!

SPIRIT 3:   Come on, you silly goose.

SCROOGE: It's him, old James! Hallo, James!

JAMES: Wait for me!

SCROOGE: James! It's me!

THE PAST: These are but shadows of the things that have
                been. They have no consciousness of us.

SCROOGE: What? And that's Eggsy, and behind him
                Tommy Traddles! And look there!

SPIRIT 4:   Wait!

SCROOGE: It's Emily. Dear, dear Emily. Poor thing.

THE PAST: Come. The school is not yet deserted. Someone
                is left there still.

The school bell rings. SCROOGE *becomes somber. They enter the
schoolyard. It's empty but for* YOUNG EBENEZER/THE BOY *sitting
upon his suitcase waiting for the coach.*

SCROOGE: It's him again. Why does he look so unpleasant?

THE PAST: Is he not familiar?

SCROOGE: He's the boy that follows me and taunts me since
                ... since ... He has no business here, he ought to
                be ...

THE PAST: Your lip trembles. Why?

SCROOGE: It's nothing. A memory maybe, the unwanted
                stirring of something long dead.

THE PAST: Look.

POSTMAN *enters.* YOUNG EBENEZER *perks up happily.*

POSTMAN: The coach passed out of town by the north road moments ago, I'm afraid. It bore these letters for a young master Scrooge? Do you know him.

SCROOGE: Scrooge? Yes . . . he's me.

POSTMAN: (*handing over the letter*) Excellent. A merry Christmas to you.

POSTMAN *exits.* YOUNG EBENEZER *opens the first letter and reads it.* FATHER *enters and recites the letter.*

FATHER: I regret that upon the circumstance of our declining financial state, we find we have more to profit by your staying at school than by your coming home for Christmas. I'm sure you would not wish hardship on your mother, and you will readily observe how your presence would be a pecuniary distress in this season.

At any rate, Christmas is time better spent on your studies than on frivolities of food and festivity that we can ill afford.

Yours affectionately, your Father.

THE PAST: That poor boy.

THE PAST *turns its light upon* SCROOGE *who stares at the* BOY *in silence and extends his hand to push the scene away.*

THE PAST: Look. There is more.

YOUNG EBENEZER *opens the other letter and* YOUNG FAN *enters, and* SCROOGE *drops his arm, stepping forward in joyful recognition.*

YOUNG FAN: My dear, brother. Father assures me that, at your school, Christmas is the merriest time of all and you're in a much better situation for joy than we are here.

SCROOGE: If only she knew the misery of it.

YOUNG FAN: And he says we may go to Marshalsea soon. That sounds wonderful to me, but by the way he says it I fear it's less wonderful than I imagine. Mother cries when she hears the name of the place. Perhaps next year you can come with us, Benny. I shall hope for it and pray. Ever your little sister, Fan.

YOUNG EBENEZER *slowly puts the letters away and pulls his case back into the schoolhouse.*

THE PAST: What's the matter.

SCROOGE: I wish . . . I wish I could . . .

THE PAST: What do you wish?

SCROOGE: It's nothing. It's too late. It doesn't matter. It's past. It's gone.

SCROOGE *turns away from the scene.*

THE PAST: Gone? Is it? Let us see another Christmas.

SCENE 6

The COMPANY *all stream out of the schoolhouse wishing one another goodbye and merry Christmas. They are older now, teens or young adults.*

SCROOGE: But years have passed.

SPIRIT 3:   When I come back I'll be heavier by ten puddings if its one.

SPIRIT 4:   Merry Christmas, Tommy. And goodbye, and a merry New Year as well.

JAMES: We'll see how tight that waistcoat fits in a month.

SPIRIT 1:   Where's Ebenezer? Pouting again at his desk?

SPIRIT 3:   He's always miserable. Never goes anywhere but to bed.

SCROOGE: Look how they've grown. How?

THE PAST: I hold the keys to many changes. Times. Places. And other things more mysterious yet.

TEEN EBENEZER *enters.*

SPIRIT 2:   There he is.

SCROOGE: There he is.

JAMES: Cheer up, Benny! Maybe they'll send you a gift.

SPIRIT 3:   Maybe it'll be a coat with no holes at the elbows!

The youths laugh and point at TEEN EBENEZER'S *tattered coat.*

SPIRIT 1 (LEAD): Or new shoes! What do you think, Benny? Will
                 you be dressed fresh and neat when we get back?

SPIRIT 3:   It'll be a Christmas miracle!

JAMES: Leave him be. Hang in there, old boy.

TEEN EBENEZER: Leave me alone.

The COMPANY *exits.*

JAMES: Well, with us gone, you'll have the place to your-
                   self and quiet besides.

TEEN EBENEZER: Good. Then no one will have to look at me.

TEEN EBENEZER *inspects his tattered coat.*

JAMES: It's not that bad, Benny . . . but a new one would
                   fit you well, there's no mistake about that. If only
                   a coat could grow to keep up with your arms.

TEEN EBENEZER *tries in vain to pull his sleeves down to cover his*
wrists.

TEEN EBENEZER: I hate it.

JAMES: Never you mind, old boy. What's a Christmas to miss anyway, hey? Nothing much. Too many people. Too little food to go around. Too many mothers and fathers looking on and making a fuss. I'd prefer it here with you any old day. What's a Christmas but a humbug, I say.

Teen Ebenezer *laughs.*

Teen Ebenezer: (*wistfully*) Humbug.

James: That's right. HumBUG, I say!

The Past: *Humbug*! How delightful!

Scrooge: James was good to me. I'd forgotten him.

James and Teen Ebenezer *laugh together.*

James: Merry Christmas, Benny.

James extends his hand for Teen Ebenezer *to shake.*

James: I shall see you in a new year and we'll make it a good one. The best one yet.

James *exits.* Teen Ebenezer *looks after him then takes off his coat, inspects its holes and throws it angrily. He sits with his head in his hands. In the distance (offstage) we hear* James *depart on the coach. Everyone there sounds happy.* Teen Ebenezer *walks dejectedly back into the school.*

The Past: Let us see another, a better year perhaps.

The lights shift and again the Company *stream out of the school wishing one another Merry Christmas.*

Spirit 3:   Don't worry, Benny. I'll bring you back a leftover pudding.

THE PAST: Ah. You've got bigger. Look at that!

EBENEZER *enters*

SCROOGE: Bigger perhaps, but yet a boy. And soon even
                 that will be gone.

SPIRIT 4:   Is Benny staying again?

THE PAST: Gone? Are you sure? You are always all yourself,
                 all at once—or you ought to be. The boy, the
                 man, the same. Don't you agree?

SCROOGE: What?

THE PAST: Nevermind. But look at him, where has he got
                 such a long face?

SPIRIT 1 (LEAD): Maybe they've forgotten all about you, Benny.
                 Do you want me to ask them?

JAMES: Let him be. Come on, Benny. Come home with
                 me this year.

EBENEZER: No. I'll wait. My sister may write. I should hate
                 to miss her letter if she does.

JAMES: As you wish. Next year, then. Merry Christmas,
                 Benny.

EBENEZER: Next year, James. I shall look forward to it.

JAMES *and* EBENEZER *shake hands. All exit and* EBENEZER *plods
back into the schoolhouse.*

THE PAST: Another. Let us see another.

SCROOGE: No, spirit. I don't want to see any more. I don't
                 want to . . .

The lights shift. The COMPANY, *again, are leaving for Christmas.*

JAMES: Come on, Benny. Are you packed?

EBENEZER: I am. I have clothes enough, I think. And a better waistcoat than last year. It's not a fine one, though. Are you sure they won't make sport of it?

JAMES: Everyone will love you. It'll be the best Christmas ever. The carriage is at the corner. Don't forget your overcoat. And your hat! Every young man needs a hat in the city!

JAMES *picks up his suitcase and exits.*

A beat. FAN *enters, older now. She looks around for* EBENEZER *until he emerges with coat and hat.*

FAN: Benny?

SCROOGE *gasps.*

SCROOGE: It's her.

EBENEZER: (*Looking off in the direction of* JAMES *and then back at* FAN.) Fan? Little Fan?

FAN: I've come to bring you home!

EBENEZER: Home?

FAN: Home, home, home.

EBENEZER: You've got so big!

FAN;   Yes! I'm big and I'm here to bring you home for good. Father sent me in the coach to fetch you.

EBENEZER: Are you sporting with me?

FAN: You are to be a man now, and to go to work at
               an office like Father and to make a wage and
               improve the family situation, he says. You are
               never to come back here again.

EBENEZER: Never? Shall I not finish school then?

FAN: School? Is that your concern?

EBENEZER: But, I was to visit with James this Christmas. His
               family has promised me a . . .

EBENEZER *looks off in the direction his friend departed.*

FAN: James? Who is this James? Listen to me, Benny!
               We're to be together all Christmas long and
               have the merriest time in all the world. Can you
               believe it?

EBENEZER: At my word, I cannot!

The two of them hug.

EBENEZER: You are quite a woman, little Fan!

FAN: I shall be Big Fan now, you'll see.

SCROOGE: You shall always be Little Fan to me. And you
               will never change.

FAN: Come with me, Benny, our coach is waiting.

EBENEZER: But wait. Fan, I . . . James?

FAN: We're here, Benny. For you. Don't you want to
               come with me?

EBENEZER: I do. Of course I do. It's only . . .

FAN: Don't you love me any more?

THE PAST: Stop!

THE PAST *stretches out its hand and the two young people freeze.*
SCROOGE *and* THE PAST *approach them.*

THE PAST: You went with her?

SCROOGE: I did. Of course I did.

THE PAST: Such a delicate creature. A breath might have
                  withered her.

SCROOGE: My sweet sister.

THE PAST: She had a large heart.

SCROOGE: So she had. Such a heart. Too big perhaps.

THE PAST: Tell me.

The COMPANY *enter.*

SCROOGE: She always loved me.

SPIRIT 1 (LEAD): She was soft.

SPIRIT 2:   And childlike.

SPIRIT 1 (LEAD): She brightened every room . . .

SPIRIT 2:   . . . and lightened every heart.

SCROOGE: She married young.

SPIRIT 1 (LEAD): So young.

THE PAST: Yet happy?

SCROOGE: So happy. Father doted on her. He gave her
                  everything.

SPIRIT 1 (LEAD): Clothes.

SPIRIT 4:   Gifts.

SCROOGE: The finest trinkets he could afford.

FATHER *hangs a locket about* FAN'*s neck.*

SPIRIT 1 (LEAD): And many he could not.

SCROOGE: We all felt the costly weight of her dowery. But
                we loved her the more for it.

THE PAST: She deserved it.

SCROOGE: My little Fan. But . . .

SPIRIT 2:   (*whispering*) The child.

SPIRIT 3:   (*whispering*) The child.

SPIRIT 1 (LEAD): (*whispering*) The child!

THE PAST: Tell me all of it. Show me!

THE PAST *shines her light on the* COMPANY *eagerly.*

SCROOGE: She died.

The COMPANY *lays* FAN *down on the stage.* SCROOGE *turns away,*
GESTURING *to push the memory away.* EBENEZER *kneels beside her,*
mourning. THE BOY *enters and does the same.*

SCROOGE: A woman, perhaps, but yet a girl. Ever a girl to
                me.

THE PAST: With such a heart.

EBENEZER *removes the locket from her neck. He kisses it and places*
it in his pocket.

SPIRIT 4: (*whispering*) The child.

THE PAST: She had children?

SCROOGE: One. Too little and too much all at once. She brought him into the world and he took her out of it—all in the same instant.

The stage goes dark. The COMPANY *exit.*

THE PAST: Your nephew?

SCROOGE: Yes. My nephew.

Shadows encroach until SCROOGE *and the* PAST *are alone.*

THE PAST: Come, my light illumines something new.

They turn and are amid the city streets.

SCENE 7

Crowds pass by, caroling. The shops are festooned with Christmas hangings. SCROOGE *and* THE PAST *approach a shop with a large frosty window, beyond which people make merry. They look in.*

THE PAST: Do you know it? Show it to me. Name it!

SCROOGE: My first situation. I was apprenticed here, and...

BELLE *enters.*

BELLE: Benny?

SCROOGE: Belle...Look at her.

THE PAST: Oh, I like her. Who was she?

THE PAST *walks around* BELLE, *shining her light and examining her curiously.*

SCROOGE: She was the brightest star in my sky, or any sky. I worked for her father, and she...

BELLE: Where are you, Benny?

SCROOGE: She and I were...

EBENEZER, *now a man, steps up behind her.*

EBENEZER: You're late.

BELLE *jumps in fright.*

BELLE: Oh you bad thing, Benny! I was helping father with his preparations. You've no reason to frighten me. And why are you still working? It's Christmas Eve!

EBENEZER: Do I frighten you, Belle?

BELLE: You couldn't frighten a mouse, Benny. But I shall let you think yourself as frightful as a ghost if it will make you happy.

EBENEZER: As a ghost?

BELLE: You are my frightfully beloved boy, and I shall quake with terror.

EBENEZER *embraces her.*

EBENEZER: Is it fright that makes you tremble now?

BELLE: This is a tremor of . . . quite another sort--but it will be fright indeed if father sees us.

BELLE *pushes him gently away.*

EBENEZER: I have something I wish to give you.

BELLE: Have you bought me a Christmas gift, Benny?

EBENEZER *removes the locket from his pocket and holds it up.* BELLE *gasps.*

BELLE: It's lovely! But how can you afford it?

EBENEZER: This was Fan's. It is all that I have left of her.

BELLE: Benny, you cannot.

EBENEZER: (*hanging it about her neck*) In all the world I can think of no other neck that I should rather bear its beauty and memory. It has only ever hung upon a beloved breast, and I would that it should do so again.

BELLE: Benny . . .

EBENEZER: I would that it should stay there. Always.

BELLE: What? Do you mean . . .

EBENEZER: I shall speak with your father soon, in a month perhaps or six if it must be, once I've made something more of myself, and . . .

BELLE: You need be nothing more for me. You are enough. We shall be penniless perhaps, but we shall be together and happy always.

EBENEZER: (taking her hand) I would be destitute indeed if I had not the riches I hold in my hand now. And I shall undertake to better myself to our good end, to the benefit of our life together.

                Come. Will you walk with me? The river is lovely this time of night.

EBENEZER *cups her face gently as if holding the most marvelous and delicate of jewels.* THE PAST *stretches out its hand.*

THE PAST: Stop.

The scene freezes and THE PAST *examines them.*

THE PAST: You loved her very much.

SCROOGE: Of course I did. I loved her as I have loved . . . nothing else.

THE PAST: But you do love something else. Something in her place, I think. What is it?

SCROOGE: Why do you show me these things, spirit. My chest is stirred and I like not the sensation of it. Return me to my chamber. Leave me be.

THE PAST: Hmm. Soon. Perhaps. Let us see another Christmas. Let us discover little more.

SCROOGE: (*extending his arm*) Please, spirit. No. Please. Let it stay hidden.

THE PAST: What is hidden cannot heal. Look.

THE PAST *lowers* SCROOGE*'s arm and shines its light upon the door.* BELLE *has exited.* FEZZIWIG *enters.*

SCROOGE: (*quietly, in wonder*) It's old Fezziwig. Bless his heart. It's Fezziwig alive again.

SCROOGE *and* THE PAST *enter the shop.*

FEZZIWIG: Look alive! Wake up! Ebenezer! Dick!

EBENEZER *and* DICK *enter, young men.*

SCROOGE: It's Dick Wilkins, right there! Bless me, yes. There he is.

FEZZIWIG: Listen to me, boys. No more work tonight. Christmas Eve, Dick. Do you understand? Christmas, Ebenezer. Do you hear? Let's have the shutters up and our work put away before a man can say Jack Robinson.

DICK *and* EBENEZER *close up the shop, drawing shutters on the windows, putting away the books, clearing the floor.*

FEZZIWIG: Clear it away, all of it. What does it matter! Let's have lots of room here. Yes, just so. Everyone will be here soon enough. There's room for all of them. Help me with this table. Move that chair. Desk in the corner. Stoke the fire. Well done, Ebenzer. Good lad. Are you ready?

The COMPANY *enters. A fiddler leaps onto the desk and plays. All dance and make merry while* SCROOGE *and* THE PAST *look on.*

SCROOGE: Why there's Mrs. Fezziwig. Look at her! And everyone else. The housemaid. The baker! And that fellow over there! He was the milliner from down the street! I'd forgotten him but there he is. There they all are. Aren't they lovely! Do you see them? All alive again, just as it should be.

BELLE *enters and tries to coax* EBENEZER *into dancing.*

SCROOGE: Aren't they all lovely.

The COMPANY *dances until . . .*

FEZZIWIG: STOP!

Everyone freezes. FEZZIWIG *pours a class of port, raises it.*

FEZZIWIG: Ebenezer, stop your slinking about in the shadows and sally forth! Belle, come here, my dear.

EBENEZER *and* BELLE *join* FEZZIWIG.

MRS. FEZZIWIG: Glasses everyone. Find a glass! You there! Pour them all up.

FEZZIWIG: Fill them full and with the finest you can find. Full to the brim and slopping over for it's such an occasion—and not only for the coming of Christmas.

FEZZIWIG *places* BELLE*'s hand in* EBENEZER*'s.*

FEZZIWIG: If all our cakes and drinks—

MRS. FEZZIWIG: —and puddings—

FEZZIWIG: —and all the expense and effort of an entire year is gone the blink of an eye for the sake of one good night among the best and brightest of souls, then it's well spent, every farthing, for its bought what cannot have a price, and I'm a richer man for being the poorer.

Everyone "here here's."

FEZZIWIG: Give me your hand, dear. Put it there and hold it steady, Ebenezer. There's a good lad. Today I am the happiest man in the world, and before the night is up I intend to make myself a good deal happier yet. For this Christmas Eve I have been given all that a father desires, and what's that? Belle, my daughter dearest and her Benny, my apt apprentice, are pledged for marriage!

Everyone applauds.

MRS. FEZZIWIG: Raise them a glass. And may God bless them.

ALL: God bless them!

Everyone drinks. FEZZIWIG *downs his whole glass.*

MRS. FEZZIWIG: Now bring me another that I may bless the good fortunes of my forthcoming grandchildren. For they shall all be spoilt with honey and biscuits till they're as fat and as happy as I am.

All laugh. The music begins again and FEZZIWIG *encourages* EBENEZER *and* BELLE *to dance. They do as all watch.*

FEZZIWIG *empties his glass, tosses it aside, and pulls* MRS. FEZZIWIG *from the crowd. The fiddler begins and the couple dance riotously to the enjoyment of all.*

FEZZIWIG: Well done! And a Merry Christmas to all!

FEZZIWIG *ushers everyone out with thanks and Merry Christmas until only* EBENEZER *and* DICK *are left.*

THE PAST: (*sighing*) A trifle and a waste, I suppose, to make these silly folks so full of gratitude.

SCROOGE: A trifle?!

THE PAST *places a finger on* SCROOGE'S *lips and motions him to listen.*

BELLE *enters.*

BELLE: Will you walk me home?

EBENEZER: I cannot. I have work to do before the night is over.

BELLE: Tonight? Of all nights? Have you not yet made enough of yourself?

EBENEZER: Of good labor is a good life built, is it not?

BELLE: Not only.

            (*beat*)

            We used to walk by the river in the evenings. Do
            you remember?

EBENEZER: The river? Why? Yes. Yes, I remember.

BELLE: Moments spent, I think—I thought—in the
            building of . . . something.

EBENEZER: I'm sorry, my love. Can we discuss your memo-
            ries of the river tomorrow? I shall come for tea in
            the afternoon.

BELLE: Come, Benny. Put all this away. What's this busi-
            ness but a humbug anyway.

EBENEZER: A humbug?

THE PAST: What did she say?

BELLE: Yes, a humbug that buzzes about and calls you
            away from better things. Let tomorrow's work
            wait for tomorrow. Walk with me. Tonight.

EBENEZER: There will be other nights to walk. There will
            always be other nights. We shall have all the
            nights in the world.

BELLE: Very well. Have your beloved humbug, and I will
            go with my father. Merry, Christmas, Benny.

EBENEZER: Merry Christmas, my love.

BELLE *exits.* EBENEZER *and* DICK *clean up and neaten the room.*

SCROOGE: You should have gone with her. Can't you see!

Go after her! What are you doing, you stupid, foolish ... boy!

THE PAST: He cannot hear you here. Would you have heard you then?

DICK: Bless old Fezziwig, his feet move faster at sixty than mine at twenty. How does he do it?

EBENEZER: With such trifles of his, he winnows our profits away by the half-penny and farthing.

THE PAST: Trifles?

DICK: Perhaps. But he has the power to render us happy or unhappy; to make our service light or burdensome, a pleasure or a toil. He wields it better than most, I think.

EBENEZER: He can only afford so much dance and drink before he's lightened all our accounts.

SCROOGE: That's the price of merriment.

DICK: But his chief wealth lies in words and looks, in things so slight and winsome that they are impossible to add and count up in a ledger. The happiness he gives is a great fortune. Is it not?

THE PAST *turns to look at* SCROOGE.

THE PAST: What's the matter?

SCROOGE: Nothing.

THE PAST: No. More than nothing, I think.

PAST shines its light directly at SCROOGE.

SCROOGE: It's nothing. Turn your light or I will cap it
                myself.

THE PAST: Come then. My time grows short. Let us find
                something more profitable to look at. Another
                Christmas. Another time. Another twinkling of
                light. Quick!

SCENE 8

JACOB *and* EBENEZER *enter and speak in hushed tones.*

EBENEZER: I don't know, Jacob. It's just that . . .

SCROOGE: Jacob Marley. Again! What's this?

JACOB: A true partnership, Benny. Between the two of us all the coin in London could be ours. Think of it! Marley & Scrooge! Or Scrooge & Marley, if you like. Up on a sign for all to see! Or do you mean to keep with Fezziwig and cuddle up with the middle class?

SCROOGE: You have no business here, Spirit!

EBENEZER: Don't go hard upon me, Jacob. Fezziwig, a silly fool though he is, has been good to me, even if . . .

JACOB: If he was good to you, he'd offer you something more bankable than his daughter! Are you a partner yet? No. All this time and you're a mere clerk on the wage of a chimneysweep. He'll be dead in a year and you'll be left with nothing but your own debt and the burden of supporting a new wife into the deal.

BELLE *enters unseen and hovers at the edge of the stage, listening.*

SCROOGE: No, no. Stop this.

JACOB: You must think about the future, Benny, think about what's yet to come! Join with me. We can be the lords of Lombard Street!

EBENEZER: Speak quietly, Jacob. Perhaps you're right. Draw up the papers and I will think on it. I will decide tomorrow.

THE PAST *turns its light on* BELLE. EBENEZER *goes to sit beside her by the fire.*

EBENEZER: My dear, what's wrong?

BELLE: It matters little, to you.

EBENEZER: What does?

SCROOGE: (*SCROOGE extends his arm to push the scene away.*) I cannot look at it!

THE PAST: Yes. Look. We may profit from it, Ebenezer Scrooge. Or is it a . . . humbug?

THE PAST *shines its light upon the scene. The spirit lowers* SCROOGE'S *arm and pushes him into the scene.* SCROOGE *and* EBENEZER *act as a single person, both engaged in conversation with* BELLE.

BELLE: I once was your idol, Benny. You sought me and valued me above all things. Or so I thought. But you are changed.

SCROOGE: Changed?

BELLE: Another idol has displaced me.

EBENEZER: Come. What is this talk? What idol has displaced you?

BELLE: A golden one.

SCROOGE: So we are come to this.

EBENEZER: Yet again.

BELLE: Come to it? We have never got beyond it.

SCROOGE: Mine was the even-handed dealing of business.

EBENEZER: There is nothing upon which the world is so hard as poverty, and there is nothing it condemns with such severity as the pursuit of wealth!

BELLE: You fear the world too much. All your other hopes have merged into the hope of being beyond the chance of its reproach. I have seen your nobler aspirations fall off one by one, until the master-passion, Gain, engrosses you. Have I not?

EBENEZER: What then? I have done it, and do it still . . .

SCROOGE: . . . for you!

EBENEZER: I am not changed towards you.

BELLE *stares at* EBENEZER *sadly.*

SCROOGE: Am I?

BELLE: Our contract is an old one. It was made when we were both poor and I content to be so until we could improve our fortune by patient industry. But now . . . you are changed.

EBENEZER: Changed? How?

BELLE: When our love was made, you were another man.

SCROOGE: (*angrily*) I was a boy!

EBENEZER: I was a boy!

BELLE: Your own manner discovers you. You are not now what you were then, and what I am still.

SCROOGE: And what is that?!

BELLE: (*approaching sadly*) Ebenezer, my Benny, that which promised happiness when we were one in heart is fraught with misery now that we are two. I have watched you change and have been helpless to stop it. How often have I tried?

SCROOGE: Try once more. Please.

BELLE: It is enough. We are two again who once were one. And I release you.

EBENEZER: Have I ever sought release?

BELLE: In words? No. Never.

SCROOGE: In what then?

BELLE: In a changed nature. In an altered spirit. In another attitude toward life and another hope as its great end.

EBENEZER: I ... I ...

BELLE: Tell me, if the first we ever met was but today, would you seek me out and try to win me now?

EBENEZER: You think not?

SCROOGE: I would. I would.

BELLE: I would gladly think otherwise if I could. But if
                 you were free today, can I believe that you would
                 choose a dowery-less girl? You, who in your very
                 confidence with her, weigh everything by Gain.

                 I release you, Benn—Ebenezer. With a full heart,
                 and for the love of him who once you were.

BELLE *turns her face from* EBENEZER.

EBENEZER: Please . . .

BELLE: The memory of the past half makes me hope you
                 will feel pain in this. But I know otherwise. A
                 very, very brief time, and you will dismiss the
                 recollection of me as an unprofitable dream, one
                 from which it happened well that you awoke.

                 May you be happy in the life you have chosen.
                 Goodbye, Ebenezer.

BELLE *removes her locket and places it on* EBENEZER'*s desk.*

SCROOGE: (*to* BELLE) Wait! Wait! No!

                 (*to* EBENEZER) Go after her, you fool!

EBENEZER GESTURES, *extends his arm toward* SCROOGE, *and
in the direction* BELLE *has exited. Then he plucks up the locket,
straightens his coat, checks his pocket watch. He seems to look directly
at* SCROOGE.

EBENEZER: (*whisper*) Humbug.

EBENEZER *walks calmly offstage in the opposite direction of* BELLE.

SCROOGE: Spirit! Show me no more! Conduct me home. Why do you delight to torture me? Whatever else you wish to show, let it remain hidden!

THE PAST: What is hidden cannot heal.

SCROOGE: I don't wish to be healed!

THE PAST: One shadow more!

SCROOGE: No more. Put out your light and give me darkness for peace!

THE PAST *evades* SCROOGE *who tries to catch it.* THE PAST *illuminates another room.*

SCENE 9

BELLE *is older, sitting by the fire and knitting.*

SCROOGE: What's this? Stop it. Where are we?

DICK *enters with an arm-full of presents.*

SCROOGE: Dick? What's he doing here?

DICK: Merry Christmas, Belle!

BELLE: What's all this! We can't possibly afford it all!

DICK *puts down the gifts.*

DICK: One for each of the children. Was everyone agreeable to the plans?

SCROOGE: This is base. Treacherous. You are a villain, spirit!

BELLE: The children will be home soon with Miss Pross. Your mother will be here for dinner at half past. And the rest will arrive soon after. Did you get cakes?

DICK: I did. And I saw an old friend on the way. Can you guess who?

SCROOGE: No. No. I don't want to know. Spirit! I can't. I won't. Don't make me.

BELLE: If you came by way of the bakery across from the counting house, I can guess.

SCROOGE: No. Spirit! Stop!

BELLE: Old Mister Scrooge.

THE PAST: These are shadows of the things that have been. That they are what they are and as you have made them, do not blame me!

DICK: I passed his office window and he had a single miserable candle inside. His partner lies upon the point of death, I hear, yet there he sat alone and counting in his books at Christmas. To think that could have been me if we'd kept in business together. Poor old Benny. He's quite alone in the whole world, I do believe.

SCROOGE: Leave me! I cannot bear it!

SCROOGE *seizes* THE PAST *and tries to force it away.*

DICK: And it could have been you too, love. What an awful fate you escaped.

BELLE: Don't be cruel, Dick. He has his own company to keep and its all he cared for in the end.

SCROOGE: NO! I will snuff you out! I will bury you!

BELLE: I pity him.

SCROOGE *takes off his coat and tries to smother out* THE PAST*'s* *light. They struggle.*

As the light flashes and ebbs. The Boy *enters and tries to stop* Scrooge *from snuffing out* The Past.

SCROOGE: Get away! I don't know you! Go away!

The last thing Scrooge *sees before he smothers out* The Past *entirely is the* Boy, Young Ebenezer, *with his arms outstretched, as if asking for help.*

SCROOGE: (*extending his arm to the* Boy) Get away!

THE PAST: (*weakly*) What is hidden cannot heal.

All goes dark, and the scene is again Scrooge's *bedroom.* Scrooge *looks around and then sits on the edge of his bed and cries. The* Company *of spirits swirl around him the in the darkness, murmuring and then slowly dissipating one by one.*

SPIRIT 4:   Was that supposed to happen?

SPIRIT 1 (LEAD): I don't know.

SPIRIT 4:   Is it done?

SCROOGE: Go away and good riddance!

SPIRIT 2:   He's broken.

SPIRIT 1 (LEAD): He feels it, but he hasn't seen.

SCROOGE: Humbug to spirits. Humbug to haunting and humbug to bygone children one and all.

SPIRIT 3:   He doesn't want to see.

SPIRIT 1 (LEAD): He must.

SPIRIT 4:   Can we make him?

SCROOGE: Give me darkness and leave me in peace!

SCROOGE *climbs into his bed and throws the covers up over his head. We can hear him whispering "Leave me be" over and over. Tick. Tock. Tick. Tock. The clock marches toward Two.*

ACT 2

SCENE 1

SCROOGE *is in bed, snoring. The clock ticks loudly. The toll of Two sounds the first time and* SCROOGE *starts upright in his bed. The company of spirits swirl in and out of the shadows to speak.*

SPIRIT 3:   (*whispered*) Can I wake him up?

SPIRIT 4:   (*whispered*) Are we ready?

SPIRIT 1 (LEAD): Wake up!

SPIRIT 2:   (*whispered*) She's coming!

SPIRIT 1 (LEAD): Ebenezer!

ALL: WAKE UP!

The COMPANY *of spirits vanish.*

SCROOGE: Wha?

He looks around in alarm.

The second toll of Two strikes.

SCROOGE: AHH!

He flops down and throws the cover over his head in fear.

Silence.

Slowly a light begins to glow in the next room, accompanied by the humming of a carol. SCROOGE *gets out of bed and tip toes to the door. As soon as he touches the knob . . .*

THE PRESENT: Come in, human. Come in and look upon me!

SCROOGE: Must I?

THE PRESENT: COME!

SCROOGE *jumps in fright but timidly obeys.*

THE PRESENT: Come in and know me better, Ebenezer Scrooge.

SCROOGE: Here I am.

THE PRESENT: I am the Ghost of Christmas Present. Am I not magnificent?

THE PRESENT *throws its arms wide and the room is showered in light. It's adorned with garland and gifts and foods of all kinds, an opulent sight.* SCROOGE *looks on in wonder.*

THE PRESENT: Hah hah hah. Have you *ever* seen the like of *me* before?

SCROOGE: Indeed I have not. Never.

THE PRESENT: But have you not walked forth with the elder brothers and sisters of my ancient family? I am but the youngest of them.

SCROOGE: Your family? I'm afraid I haven't. Have you many siblings?

THE PRESENT: (*laughing*) More than eighteen hundred since the first of us, and he was great indeed. Never before had the earth seen his like, and never since. But we all are born to recall the world into the birthright it has forgotten. Do you understand me, human?

SCROOGE: I've understood little enough since the sun gave me over to this cursed night.

THE PRESENT: (*laughing*) Cursed?!

SCROOGE: More than eighteen hundred brothers and sisters, you say? That seems a tremendous number to provide for. Especially if you are all so large.

THE PRESENT: (*intimidating*) Large? Look on me now and you see but a splinter of an oak. My kin are the heralds of an age you have scarcely dreamt of, and in all the tongues of your mortal kind there are not words enough to circumscribe the size and weight and import of my family and I. We are Joy's unending lodestone. And we are titan!

SCROOGE: (*cowering*) Yes, I see that you are. And I feel some strange engine stirring within me. Therefore, if you have aught to teach me, let me profit by it and be done.

THE PRESENT: Come then, human. Catch upon my robe and hold it fast. I have much to show!

THE PRESENT *lifts its glowing stave and brings it down on the stage. The light flickers.*

SCENE 2

The light steadies and SCROOGE *and* THE PRESENT *are on a common city street where common people go about their daily business with merry greetings.*

As they walk amongst the crowd, whenever THE PRESENT *touches someone with its glowing stave, they are changed for the better. The* BEGGAR *that* SCROOGE *shunned earlier enters.*

THE PRESENT: Witness this poorly beggar. Watch, and see what will happen.

LONDONER 1 *walks past the beggar in rags.*

SPIRIT 4: She'll bless the beggar and make him rich, won't she?

SPIRIT 1 (LEAD): Just wait. And watch.

SPIRIT 3: No. Wait? But why is she . . .

THE PRESENT *blesses* LONDONER 1, *who turns and empties coins into the* BEGGAR's *hands.*

BEGGAR: Thank you, sir! Bless you!

SPIRIT 2:   Look out, someone else is coming.

SCROOGE: What are you doing?

LONDONER 2 *passes the* BEGGAR, *the spirit blesses her, and she turns and invites the* BEGGAR *to dinner.*

LONDONER 2:   Are you hungry? Come with me, love. We've room for you at my dinner table tonight.

LONDONER 2 *hands the* BEGGAR *an address card and departs.*

SPIRIT 2:   I didn't see that coming.

SCROOGE: But wouldn't it be easier just to toss him a tuppence?

THE PRESENT: Easier? What has ease to do with the welfare of another?

As the BEGGAR *stands,* THE PRESENT *blesses* LONDONER 3 *passing by who offers the* BEGGAR *a coat.*

LONDONER 3:   The weather is frigid, my good man. Will you take my coat? I'm sure I can find another.

SCROOGE: That's preposterous. Now he doesn't have a coat.

As the BEGGAR *begins to exit, now upright and respectable in a coat,* THE PRESENT *blesses* LONDONER 4 *who offers the* BEGGAR *a job.*

LONDONER 4:   You sir, are you employed? I have work. I can offer you a reasonable wage.

BEGGAR: No, sir. I mean, thank you, sir.

SCROOGE: Only a fool would hire a man without a vetted reference.

Londoner 4:   Good man, come see me tomorrow on Baker
                Street!

Scrooge *and* The Present *look into a window where the beggar
is welcomed to the feast table with the* Londoners.

The Present: But do you see how readily the world might
                change? For all the ruin wrought by humankind,
                it all might alter in a twinkling. It's only bent
                lines that show out shapes of grace, and so over
                the bent world we spirits brood, in search of a
                place to set a lovely curve. Do you see?

Scrooge: You are mysterious, Spirit.

The Present: Look upon the mended world glimpsed here
                in a meal. They feast on joy itself, and later they
                will lay in the cool of the evening to dream of the
                brown brink where morning eastward springs.

The Present *blesses the feast with her stave.*

Scrooge: Is there some peculiar flavor in what you give
                them from your stave?

The Present: There is. My own. And there is no other like it,
                nor so sweet.

Scrooge: But would it apply to any kind of dinner on this
                day?

The Present: To any kindly given. And to a poor one most of
                all.

Scrooge: Why to a poor one most?

The Present: Because it needs it most.

SCROOGE: It makes me wonder, then, why you cramp these people's opportunities of innocent enjoyment.

THE PRESENT: I!?

SCROOGE: You close up the shops and the places of enjoyment, and they are left hungry in the street. You close the merry places on Sunday. Do you not?

THE PRESENT: I do this?!

SCROOGE: It's done in your name, or at least in that of your family.

THE PRESENT: (*thundering*) There are some upon this earth who lay claim to know us—those who do their deeds of pride, ill-will, hatred, envy, bigotry, and selfishness in our name—yet those are as strange to me and my kin as if they had never lived.

SCROOGE: I meant no offense, Spirit. I have always wondered.

THE PRESENT: Charge their doings upon them, and not on us. Judge not the wonder by the cracked reflection of its mirror. My kin and I, we are menders of the earth!

SCROOGE: Forgive me.

THE PRESENT: But do you see?

SCROOGE: I ... I think so.

THE PRESENT: Do you see!?

SCROOGE: I see. I try.

THE PRESENT: Come then, let us set about the work of mending.

SCENE 3

THE PRESENT *approaches the window of a home and touches it with her stave. The home is* BOB's.

THE PRESENT: Here is a needful place, human. Look you now and know it.

SCROOGE *and* THE PRESENT *enter the home and watch from a corner.*

MRS. CRATCHIT: What has ever got your precious father then? And your brother, Tiny Tim! And Martha warn't as late last Christmas Day by half-an-hour. Peter, get the dishes out, will you. And, Belinda, help your brother.

PETER: Yes, mother.

BELINDA: Do I have to?

BOB *enters with* TINY TIM *on his crutch.* MARTHA *hides behind them.*

MRS. CRATCHIT: You've come just in time, dear!

PETER: There's such a goose in the oven, Papa! Can you smell it?

MRS. CRATCHIT: Have you found our Martha? I've seen not a hair of her head.

MARTHA *pops into sight. And* BOB *laughs like a magician pulling a rabbit from a hat.*

BOB: So I have. And what father could ask for a better Christmas gift.

MRS. CRATCHIT: (*kissing* MARTHA) Why, bless your heart alive, dear, how late you are!

MARTHA: We'd a deal of work to finish up last night at the factory, and had to clear away the last of it this morning. I'm sorry I'm late, mother.

MRS. CRATCHIT: Well! Never mind so long as you are come. Sit you down before the fire, my dear, and warm you up, Lord bless you!

MARTHA: Happy Christmas, mother.

BELINDA: Happy Christmas, Martha!

MRS. CRATCHIT: And how did little Tim behave at the doctor?

BOB: As good as gold and better. He told me coming home that he hoped all the people saw him because he was a cripple, and it might be pleasant to them to remember upon Christmas Day who made lame beggars walk and blind men see.

SCROOGE: Is the boy gravely sick, Spirit?

THE PRESENT: Keep silent and watch.

MRS. CRATCHIT: (*hugging* TINY TIM) That's my lovely dear.

TINY TIM: I'm hungry.

BOB: (*with a troubled look at* MARTHA *and a somber head shake*) But neverminding that, the doctor says he's growing fine hearty and strong. Isn't that right, Tim?

TINY TIM: Hearty and strong, Papa. I'll be Tall Tim one day and tiny no more.

BOB: Strong boy. Come give your Papa a hug. And maybe next month we'll get that medicine.

BELINDA: Why does Papa look sad, Mama?

MRS. CRATCHIT: Sit down, sit down.

Everyone sits about the table piled with food.

PETER *enters with a tiny goose upon a large platter and sets it on the table.*

BOB: (*standing*) Quiet now. Quiet. I know it's not much we have, but it's more than many. And I wish it were more and mayhap one day it will be. But today, I got all I need and I wouldn't be a farthing happier if it were all in the world.

                 A Merry Christmas to us all, my dears. God bless us!

ALL: A Merry Christmas and God bless us!

TINY TIM: God bless us every one.

BOB: (*near tears*) Now eat up, my lad. Strong and hearty.

Bob serves TINY TIM's *plate and the family eats. The other children move part of their portions to* TINY TIM's *plate.*

PETER: You can have mine, Tim. I don't care for it.

TINY TIM: Thank you, Peter.

BELINDA: And some of mine as well. Martha will bake us a cake later and I'll fill up on that.

TINY TIM: Thank you, Belinda! It's such a goose, mother!

MRS. CRATCHIT: Eat up, dear. Strong and hearty.

BOB *eats nothing at all. Then* TINY TIM *looks toward* SCROOGE.

SCROOGE: Spirit, tell me. Will Tiny Tim live?

THE PRESENT *taps her stave upon the stage and the Cratchit scene freezes.*

THE PRESENT: Why, human? Does he recall you to something?

SCROOGE: Recall me? N . . . No. Or maybe. I saw a boy upon my stoop and he was strange, and seemed all about him sad. He haunts me. Was it him? Was it Tim?

THE PRESENT: Tiny Tim is not the boy who haunts you, human. But he may yet. I see a vacant seat at the table, and a crutch without an owner carefully preserved upon the mantle. If these shadows remain unaltered, this child will die.

SCROOGE: No, no. He doesn't deserve it. A boy deserves happiness doesn't he?

THE PRESENT: Every child is deserving of joy, though not all will find it. If these shadows remain unaltered by the Future, none other of my kin will find him here.

SCROOGE: No. Are you certain?

THE PRESENT: But what of it? If he be like to die he had better do it, and decrease the surplus population.

SCROOGE *backs away in horror.*

THE PRESENT: Come, human. Look on him. See. And then decide who shall live and who shall die! Will you dare it in my presence?

SCROOGE *shakes his head.*

THE PRESENT: It may be that in the sight of Heaven you are less fit to live than millions upon millions like this poor child.

SCROOGE: I didn't mean . . . I only meant to say that . . .

THE PRESENT: Oh to hear the insect pronouncing life and death among his hungry brothers in the dust! But look, human, and see how you are judged.

THE PRESENT *taps her stave again and the scene resumes.*

MRS. CRATCHIT: And bless the doctor and his medicines!

PETER: And bless the goose as well!

BELINDA: I want to bless something too!

MARTHA: Enough of blessing, or we will eat our dinner cold.

BOB: Mr. Scrooge! Before we taste the bounty, I'll give you Mr. Scrooge, the Founder of the Feast!

MRS. CRATCHIT: The Founder of the Feast indeed! I wish I had him here. I'd give him a piece of my mind to feast upon, and I hope he'd have a good appetite for it.

BOB: My dear, the children! Christmas Day.

MRS. CRATCHIT: It could only be Christmas Day, I am sure, on which one drinks the health of such an odious, stingy, hard, unfeeling man as Mr. Scrooge. You know he is, Robert! Nobody knows it better than you do!

BOB: My dear. Christmas Day.

MRS. CRATCHIT: I'll drink his health for your sake and the Day's—not for his.

Long life to him! A merry Christmas and a happy new year! He'll be very merry and very happy, I have no doubt!

ALL: Mr. Scrooge!

TINY TIM: God bless 'im!

The family continues to eat and THE PRESENT *touches them each tenderly with her stave. When she approaches* TINY TIM, TIM *seems to see the* THE PRESENT *and smile at her.*

SCROOGE: He saw you!

THE PRESENT: He did.

SCROOGE: But how? I thought . . .

THE PRESENT: He wavers upon the brink. He is so close he perceived me through the veil. The lightest breath may tip his scale toward life . . . or death.

The smallest kindness may yet heal. Or else the smallest slight may harm beyond all healing.

SCROOGE *steps softly toward* TINY TIM *and begins to reach toward him.*

THE PRESENT: Good. You begin to see. But to begin only is not enough, and the glad first footsteps of the journey have not yet been tested against the steeper climb to come. Will you continue with me, human?

SCROOGE: I am afraid, but I will try.

THE PRESENT: Good. Then brace yourself. You have seen the near. Now we shall see afar. Catch hold and fly with me and the vast distances of earth will contract to moments.

Scrooge turns away and takes hold of THE PRESENT *as the* COM-PANY *of spirits swarm around them.*

SCENE 4

SCROOGE *and* THE PRESENT *ascend into the air.*

SPIRIT 1 (LEAD): Up they fly! Until the firmament is all about them.

SPIRIT 2: Clouds like fellow travelers pass.

SPIRIT 1 (LEAD): Swiftly they soar on the backs of arctic zephyrs, and down they settle on a barren land. A land of sand and dune ...

SPIRIT 2: ... of wind and lizard ...

SPIRIT 3: ... heat-soaked and rain-parched.

SPIRIT 1 (LEAD): The sun gathers low in the west and glowers there over desolation.

SCROOGE: What place is this?

THE PRESENT: A place of bitter toil and tears and endless dust where miners delve in the deeps. Look!

SPIRIT 1 (LEAD): They pass as vapor through the rock beneath their feet. Into the hot, dark regions where iron . . .

SPIRIT 2:   . . . and copper . . .

SPIRIT 3:   . . . and tin . . .

SPIRIT 1 (LEAD): . . . and gem are gestated in the dark womb of
the world.

SPIRIT 2:   Where hewers of stone and swingers of pick . . .

SPIRIT 1 (LEAD): . . . midwife the raw material of industry and
deliver it up to the profit of humankind.

A group of miners gathers around a dim light. They hum a tune.

SCROOGE: Why, Spirit. Why do you show me these?

THE PRESENT: Because here, even in the deep places, lit only by
the false light of men, they know me. Listen.

MINER 1:   (*coughing*) Gather 'round, boys.

MINER 2:   Leave off them picks and sit.

MINER 1:   (*pouring drinks from a bottle*) Have a draught of
this was made in greener climes.

THE PRESENT *stretches out her stave and blesses the cup.*

MINER 3:   (*drinking*) An ounce of gold, that is. And a merry
Christmas in it.

The MINERS *drink.*

MINER 1:   Raise it for me missus and the small ones sad at
home without me.

The MINERS *drink again.*

MINER 3:   And again for his darlin' Darla, who we know is happy at home without 'im.

Laughter.

MINER 2:   And once more yet for a rich lode and a passage home.

MINER 3:   Lone and lorn creatures are we.

MINER 1:   Lone and lorn.

MINER 2:   And on such a day as Christmas, we're less lone and less lorn . . .

MINER 1:   . . . and yet more of both than ever.

MINER 2:   God bless them we a'long to see.

MINER 1:   God bless 'em every one.

The MINERS *return to their song and their picks. They continue humming as they exit.*

THE PRESENT: Catch up my robe, human. We cannot tarry!

SPIRIT 1 (LEAD): So slipping up through stone and earth, they pass along the backs of winds once more.

SPIRIT 3:   Soaring . . .

SPIRIT 1 (LEAD): . . . like spirits of old, brooding over the darkness of the earth.

SPIRIT 2:   Lightning forks and drives the clouds from their path!

SPIRIT 1 (LEAD): Nature kneels before the spirit and clears the way before her as she flashes across the sky.

SCROOGE: (*terrified*) Where do you take me, Spirit?

THE PRESENT *laughs.*

SPIRIT 1 (LEAD): They've crossed the last of the land and now . . .

SCROOGE: Not the sea!

THE PRESENT: (*laughing*) The sea! Hold fast, human!

SPIRIT 2:   The clash of angry waters rolls . . .

SPIRIT 3:   . . . and rages.

SPIRIT 1 (LEAD): Yet a beacon circles bright.

SPIRIT 2:   The hopeful gleam of its eye guiding ships clear of fatal reefs and sunken rocks.

SPIRIT 1 (LEAD): And here, stricken by gale and staggered by waves . . .

SPIRIT 2:   Two keep watch.

SPIRIT 1 (LEAD): Two small and alone amid the crashing of the great waters of the world.

In the light of the beacon, two lighthouse watchmen pour themselves a grog as THE PRESENT *and* SCROOGE *alight beside them and watch.* THE PRESENT *blesses their draught.*

WATCHMAN 1: We keeps Christmas as we keeps the light!

WATCHMAN 2: May they never go dim, neither one!

WATCHMAN 1: To Christmas, light o' the darkening world!

WATCHMAN 2: God bless it.

WATCHMAN 1: Come! Let us sing out a gale to answer a gale and drown out the sound of the sea.

The WATCHMEN *sing their shanty (any appropriate song), as* THE PRESENT *blesses their communion with her stave. As the song continues in humming, they fly on.*

THE PRESENT: Come. Hold to me!

SPIRIT 1 (LEAD): Much they see, and far they fly, and many homes they favor . . .

SPIRIT 4:   . . . always with a happy end.

SPIRIT 3:   The Spirit stands beside the sick of heart, and they are cheerful.

SPIRIT 1 (LEAD): The Spirit stands with people lost in foreign lands, and they are close at home.

SPIRIT 3:   They kneel low by struggling men, and men are patient in their greater hope.

SPIRIT 1 (LEAD): By poverty, and it is rich.

SPIRIT 4:   In the almshouses . . .

SPIRIT 2:   . . . *in hospitals* . . .

SPIRIT 4:   . . . and jails.

SPIRIT 3:   In misery's every refuge . . .

SPIRIT 1 (LEAD): . . . the Spirit leaves her blessing and the world is . . .

SPIRIT 4:   For a moment . . .

SPIRIT 1 (LEAD): . . . a glimmer of its greater end.

THE PRESENT: Do you see? Upon this night I visit them with gentle glimpses of the crooked tale set straight and they know me, human! They all know me! Do you see?

SCROOGE: I am shaken, but I see.

THE PRESENT: But keep close, for I am not the only one who is known tonight!

SPIRIT 1 (LEAD): And in a flash, dear old London is again about them.

SCENE 5

SCROOGE *and* THE PRESENT *enter a sitting room where* FRED *and friends are gathered. The party laugh at an unheard comment as they enter.*

FRIEND 1:   He can't have. Is that what he actually said?

FRED: He said that Christmas was a humbug, as I live and breath! He believed it too!

CLARA: It's shameful. I don't know how you can tolerate him.

FRED: I grant you he's not so pleasant as he might be, but his nature carries its own punishment.

CLARA: Punished or not, he is very rich, Fred. At least you always tell me so.

FRED: And what of it? His wealth is of no use to him. He does no good with it. He doesn't make himself comfortable with it. And he hasn't the satisfaction of thinking he's ever going to benefit us with it.

Everyone laughs.

CLARA: I have no patience with him.

The party agrees and says so.

FRED: Don't be cruel.

                I couldn't be angry with him if I tried. Who
                suffers by his ill nature and outlooks? Himself,
                always.

CLARA: Himself and as many of us as he can drag along
                with him!

FRED: Yes. He takes it into his head to dislike us, and
                he won't come and dine with us. But what's the
                consequence? He loses a dinner, and not much
                of one at that.

Everyone pauses a beat and then . . .

CLARA: I think he loses a very good dinner, thank you
                very much.

Everyone laughs and congratulates CLARA *on the quality and
quantity of the dinner.*

FRED: I didn't mean anything by it, dear. I only meant
                to say that—

CLARA: Oh, do go on, Fred! He never has enough to
                say! Has anyone else noticed? Such a ridiculous
                fellow!

Laughter.

FRED: I was only going to say that the consequence of his
                refusal is that he loses some pleasant moments—

which could do him no harm. Nevertheless, I
mean to give him the same chance every year,
whether he likes it or not.

CLARA: I pity him.

FRED: He may rail at Christmas till he dies, but he can't
                help thinking better of it if he finds me going to
                him, year after year, and saying "Uncle Scrooge!
                How are you? Will you come and dine with us?"

FRIEND 1:   If it only puts him in the vein to leave his poor
                clerk fifty pounds, that's something.

FRED: I think perhaps I shook his resolve yesterday.

CLARA: (*rolling her eyes*) I'm sure he was quite shaken,
                my love.

FRED: Fine. I've said my peace and there's an end to
                it. Wasn't there to be a desert with that most
                magnificent dinner?

FRIEND 1:   Desert?

FRIEND 2:   Let us be blessed with puddings!

CLARA: Very well, we shall have a pudding that even Fred
                cannot pity.

CLARA *goes to the side table and brings a steaming dish to the table
and serves.*

FRIEND 1:   Let's have a game before Fred finds himself too
                melancholy for good fun. Shall we play blind
                man's bluff?

FRIEND 2:   Not again. I always lose and you know it.

FRED: What about "How, When, Where?" We haven't played that one since we were at Aunt Betsie's years ago.

CLARA: I've got it. Let's do "Yes and No."

Everyone but Fred claps. He shrugs.

CLARA: It's all right, dear. You can have your way next time. Sit down and eat your pudding like a good boy.

FRIEND 2:   Who will begin?

CLARA: I've got one. I'll go first and Fred must guess. I'll give him a moment to ready his wits while I fetch drinks.

Everyone agrees.

SCROOGE: We played this one at school when . . . when I was a boy. I was a great talent at the guessing.

THE BOY *enters and stands beside* SCROOGE, *mimicking him.*

SCROOGE: I loved all manner of games, you know. Jumping rope. Hopscotch. The Whip and Top. Hoop and Stick.

THE PRESENT: (*looking tenderly at* SCROOGE *and* THE BOY *who is watching the game with rapt attention*) That boy had all the guessing and games in the world before him. My siblings tell me it was true and he knew them well.

CLARA: Very well, Fred. The game is on.

FRED: Is it an animal?

CLARA: Oh yes! A beast!

FRED: Has it four legs or two?

FRIEND 2:   It's YES or NO, Fred.

FRIEND 1:   You see, he'll spoil it.

FRED: Has it four legs then?

CLARA: No.

SCROOGE: Ask her if it has feathers!

FRED: Does it talk?

CLARA: No.

            (*aside*) It growls.

FRED: Does it eat meat?

CLARA: Hmmm. No. (No one's ever seen it to eat.)

FRED: You're making a game of me.

CLARA: I am not.

SCROOGE: Oh, oh, ask her if it's an insect!

FRED: It goes about on two legs, growling, but never
            eating?

FRIEND 1:   I know it!

FRED: You do not.

FRIEND 2:   Ask her another!

FRED: Very well. Is this creature of nightmare real or
            imagined?

CLARA: YES or NO! (But it is quite real.)

SCROOGE: What can it . . . I know it. I think I know it. Oh
              if they could hear me.

FRED: I give it up. You're making sport of me! What is
              it?

A beat for effect.

CLARA: It walks about London like this. And it grouses
              and growls and it never has anything whatever to
              do with a dinner.

FRIEND 2:   It's your Uncle Scrooooooge.

*Everyone but FRED falls over laughing. After a moment, FRED gives
in and joins them in wails of laughter. They all mimic her impression and fall into their seats out of breath. SCROOGE is dumbstruck.
THE BOY backs away into shadow.*

SCROOGE: Take me away, Spirit. I can watch no longer.
              Torment me no more.

*SCROOGE hides his face, but THE PRESENT reaches out and turns
him by the chin to make him watch.*

THE PRESENT: Watch.

FRED: He's given us plenty of merriment, I am sure, and
              it would be ungrateful not to drink his health.
              Here is a glass of mulled wine ready at hand, and
              I say, "Uncle Scrooge!"

ALL: Uncle Scrooge!

FRED: A Merry Christmas and a Happy New Year to
              the old creature, whatever he is! He wouldn't

take it from me, but may he have it, nevertheless.

CLARA: (*kissing him in apology*) Very well, then. Uncle
                   Scrooge!

THE PRESENT *waves her arm and the scene vanishes into darkness.*

SCENE 6

When THE PRESENT *turns back to* SCROOGE *and approaches, she is feeble and stumbles.*

SCROOGE: Leave me be, Spirit.

THE PRESENT: My time grows short. My life thins.

SCROOGE: You said you were eternal. Is this some new game?

THE PRESENT: My existence on this globe is short. But the length of a single night.

SCROOGE: Only one night?

THE PRESENT: Have you understood nothing, human? I end tonight amid the tolling of bells.

The bell tolls once.

THE PRESENT: Hark! My last moments draw nigh. I could not show you all if you were a hundred nights in my company, but you have seen much, and you will see one thing more.

THE PRESENT'*s robe ripples and a thin arm stretches from it's folds.* SCROOGE *starts in alarm.*

SCROOGE: What is that?

THE PRESENT: It might be a claw for all the flesh there is upon it.

THE PRESENT *parts her robe and two small children emerge. A boy and a girl. Both dirty and emaciated. They fall to the floor at the spirit's feet and cling to her robe.*

THE PRESENT: Look on them, human, and remember the sight. Blazon it upon your mind.

SCROOGE: Are they your children?

THE PRESENT: They are the offspring of humankind, yet they cling to me and plead for better fathers, better mothers, to ease their suffering along the passage to the grave.

THE PRESENT *kneels and caresses the cheek of each child in turn.*

THE PRESENT: The boy is Ignorance. The girl is Want. Look on them, and do not turn away.

SCROOGE: Is he the boy that haunts me upon my stoop? That haunts me even here?

THE PRESENT: You begin to understand, human. But that boy is another. Him you already know and have always known. Though he is no stranger to these.

SCROOGE: They stare at me with such hungry eyes. Turn them away!

THE PRESENT: Listen to me, Ebenezer Scrooge. Look on upon these brittle bones and keep their images ever before you! Fear them. Beware them both. But most of all beware this boy, for on his brow I see that written which is Doom . . . unless the writing be erased.

The bell tolls once more.

SCROOGE: (*extending his arm*) Why do you show me these awful things?

THE PRESENT: What is hidden cannot heal.

SCROOGE: And how might that writing be be erased, Spirit? Have they no refuge? Have they no resource?

Gathering the children up and stepping back into the darkness and the bell of the clock tolls . . .

THE PRESENT: Are there no prisons? Are there no workhouses?

The echo of SCROOGE *saying, "If he is like to die, he had better do it and decrease the surplus population."*

SCENE 7

The bell tolls THREE *as* SCROOGE *covers his ears and moans pitifully.*

SPIRIT 1 (LEAD): (*whispered*) It's coming.

SPIRIT 4:   (*whispered*) What is it?

SPIRIT 3:   (*whispered*) The last.

SPIRIT 1 (LEAD): (*whispered*) It's here. Hush.

The sound of wind arises, as of it blowing across a great desolation. The lights reveal the form of a figure emerging from shadow. YET TO COME *is shrouded in black. The spirit drifts across the stage to stand before* SCROOGE *in reproachful silence.*

SCROOGE: The Past has dimmed, the Present fades. And I am in the shadow now of what is Yet to Come?

YET TO COME *does not answer but slowly raises its arm to point into the distance.*

SCROOGE: Spirit. Speak. Are you are here to show me shadows of things that have not yet happened, but will happen in the time before us?

Yet to Come *answers with a single inclination of its head.*

Again the hand points.

SCROOGE: I fear you, Specter. I fear you more than any
                 spirit I have seen. Therefore show me what you
                 will, and I will attempt to find its meaning.

                 Will you not speak to me?

Yet to Come *does not move or respond, but continues pointing
into the distant darkness.*

SCROOGE: Then show me! Time is precious to me now as
                 never it was before. Unveil whatever dread sight
                 you have come to bestow.

Across the stage a scene of LONDONERS *on the street. They are carrying furniture into a warehouse. Chairs. A desk. A table, etc. They
are also carrying a sign, the front of which faces away from* SCROOGE
at all times. It reads: SCROOGE & MARLEY.

LONDONER 1:   No, I don't know much about it, either way. I
                 suppose its up to the lawyers to fight over all this
                 whatnot from 'is office.

LONDONER 2:   When did he die?

LONDONER 1:   Last night, I believe.

LONDONER 2:   Is he got no family?

LONDONER 1:   None that has any care for the insides of a
                 counting house, I reckon.

LONDONER 3:   (*stuffing his/her nose with snuff*) What was it killed 'im?

LONDONER 2:   Do I look like 'is doctor?

LONDONER 3:   I thought he'd never die.

LONDONER 1:   (*dispassionately*) God knows.

LONDONER 3:   What's he done with 'is money?

LONDONER 1:   Left it to 'is own ghost, I s'pose. He hasn't left it to me. That's all I know.

Laughter.

LONDONER 1:   Watch yourself. That sign'll fetch a pretty price if you get it lettered new. Cruncher over on Budge Row can do it for you on the cheap.

LONDONER 2:   It's likely to be a cheap funeral, too, for upon my life I don't know of anybody to go to it. S'pose we make up a party and volunteer?

LONDONER 3:   I'll go twice if a there's a lunch.

LONDONER 2:   I'll fetch the whole family if there's but a morsel to fight over!

Another laugh.

LONDONER 1:   Well, I never wear black and I never eat lunch, but I'll go for the curiosity, if anybody else will.

A clock chimes the hour.

LONDONER 2:   I'll be late if I'm not quick. I'm off.

LONDONER 1:   As am I. Good morning.

LONDONER 2:   Off with you all and good bye.

SCROOGE: Who were they? I don't understand.

The group exits as COLLECTOR 1 *&* 2 *enter.* YET TO COME *points to direct* SCROOGE'*s attention.*

SCROOGE: Ah, I know them! I saw them only yesterday!

COLLECTOR 1:   (*sighing at the sight of the counting house door*) I suppose we owe it to ourselves at least to try.

COLLECTOR 2:   That wretched door is a waste time, and this year more than last.

COLLECTOR 1:   I can scarcely imagine a return so grim as we had last year.

COLLECTOR 1:   You needn't imagine it. Grim is as grim does. Old Scratch has reaped his own at last.

COLLECTOR 2:   Has he?

COLLECTOR 1:   Indeed he has. And I daresay the world's better off.

                (*shuddering*) Colder here, isn't it?

COLLECTOR 2:   More than is seasonable. It's his shadow upon us. Chilled, like as if the place is haunted by his hollow soul.

COLLECTOR 1:   Pick up your heels, and let's try the next one. No reason to darken this door now or never again.

COLLECTOR 1:   Much good it did anyone or anything.

The COLLECTORS *exit.*

SCROOGE: Why do you show me these things? What do the affairs of strangers have to do with me?

YET TO COME *points again. A group of dingy beggars and thieves enter and begin to scavenge valuables from a musty bedroom. The bed is curtained.* MRS. DILBER *is among them.*

SCROOGE: It's Mrs. Dilber! She cleans my house on Thursdays! But what's she doing in such a place as this?

THIEF: Oh 'ere's a nice one! Look what odds I got! And what ends!

MRS. DILBER: Enough to go around, I reckon. The man took care of hisself and that's for certain.

THIEF: He won't miss it no more.

MRS. DILBER: That he won't.

THIEF: Who's worse for the loss of a few things like these? Not a dead man, on my honor.

MRS. DILBER: (*rolling her eyes*) On your "honor"? If he'd been natural with anyone in 'is lifetime, he'd have had somebody to look after him when he was struck with Death, instead of lying gasping out his last all alone by hisself.

THIEF: It's the truest word that ever was spoke.

MRS. DILBER: It's a judgment on him.

THIEF: Look 'ere, Old Joe. Make an account of it for us.

OLD JOE: Let's see what you got?

Old Joe *opens the* Thief's *bundle for all to see. It contains a few household items and some small valuables.*

OLD JOE: This'll get a fair price. A few of the others too. Oooh, look at this, hey?

MRS. DILBER: Here's the real take, Joe. Look it 'ere, tell it like it is. It's a haul of fineries and luxury if I ever seen it.

MRS. DILBER *pulls down the bed curtains.*

OLD JOE: Curtains?

MRS. DILBER: Aye! Bed-curtains! Fine and silk and they comes from somewhere you can't get to but with ships.

OLD JOE: And you haulin' 'em down, rings and all, with him lying there.

MRS. DILBER: And why not?

OLD JOE: (*whistling*) You were born to make your fortune, and you'll stop at nothin' to do it.

MRS. DILBER: I shan't hold back my hand, when I can get something by reaching it out, especially for the sake of such a tightened up old man as he was, I promise you, Joe.

Don't drop the blankets, now.

OLD JOE: His blankets, too?

MRS. DILBER: He's as cold now as a body can get and won't get no colder without 'em, I dare say.

OLD JOE: I hope he didn't die of nothing catching?

MRS. DILBER: Don't you be afraid of that. Ah! You may look

through that shirt till your eyes ache, but you won't find a hole in it, nor a threadbare spot.

OLD JOE: Never can be too sure of a garment.

MRS. DILBER: He never suffered a garment to have a hole and he spent a fortune on the mending of 'em. Thought folk would laugh to see 'is elbow through a coat sleeve! Nevermind we was all laughing at 'im for the beastly thing he was behind all that finery and coin. Anyway, it's a fine shirt, and they'd have wasted it, if it hadn't been for me.

OLD JOE: What do you call wasting of it?

MRS. DILBER: Putting it on him to be buried in. He can't look no uglier now he's without it.

SCROOGE: This is a distasteful business, Spirit. I knew the woman as an efficient cleaner of houses, but of this business I am innocent. I've seen enough.

OLD JOE: And this is a fine thing indeed.

OLD JOE *lifts up a locket.*

MRS. DILBER: Aye, that's a treasure sure.

SCROOGE: That's mine! She's stealing from her employers, the living and the dead! She's a villain!

MRS. DILBER: He used to hold it and rub when he thought I couldn't see 'im. It was that way with all 'is nice things. He kept 'em hid where they couldn't do nobody no good. I reckon it's worth a shilling.

OLD JOE: That much? I'll give you a half and not a pence further. It may have been worth something to him, but it's a trifle to anyone else.

SCROOGE: A trifle! No. Please. Make her return it!

                (*To* MRS. DILBER)

                How dare you! Thief. Thief!

MRS. DILBER: A half then it is. I'll take it and it'll be the best
                I ever did for him to drink its worth in cheap
                wine.

Everyone laughs and they scuttle offstage with their goods.

SCROOGE: An awful woman! I thank you, Spirit. I shall dismiss her at the earliest opportunity. You need show me no more.

YET TO COME *extends its hand again and points to the bed in the
shadows upon which lies a thin body covered by a sheet. Wind howls
over the desolate scene.*

SCROOGE: Merciful Heaven, no.

*Scrooge creeps toward the bed timidly but falls to his knees halfway
there and turns to implore* YET TO COME.

SCROOGE: I cannot look. Don't make me.

YET TO COME *glides to the bedside and points directly to the covered
head of the body. The spirit inclines its head toward* SCROOGE *and
then toward the body.*

SCROOGE: Spirit, this is a fearful place. If we leave it, I shall
                not leave its lesson, trust me. Let us go!

YET TO COME *is unmoved, and points still at the body's head.*
SCROOGE *tries to obey, but at the moment of uncovering the face,
relents.*

SCROOGE: I have not the power, Spirit. I have not the power.
                  My hands will not answer!

YET TO COME *is unmoving, pointing still. The company of spirits*
swirl about SCROOGE.

COMPANY: What is hidden cannot heal.

SCROOGE: If there is any person, who feels emotion caused
                  by this man's death, show that person to me,
                  Spirit, I beg you!

MRS. CRATCHIT: (*through tears*) We would have sent for you before, but we have had so little . . . this is all that's left.

MRS. CRATCHIT *offers the doctor a handful of coins.*

DOCTOR: Keep what you have. You will need it more than I.

DOCTOR *exits.* MRS. CRATCHIT *tries to comfort* BOB, *but he backs away and shuffles slowly into* TINY TIM'S *room. The boy lies dead upon the bed with the sheet pulled over him, just as the previous bed and body shown to* SCROOGE. *This bed however is surrounded by toys and beloved things and is showered in golden light.* BOB *sits next to his son and cries.*

MARTHA: Is Tiny Tim gone, mama?

MRS. CRATCHIT *nods.*

PETER: Will papa be all right. Why does he move so slowly?

MRS. CRATCHIT: I have known him walk with . . . I have known him walk with Tiny Tim upon his shoulder very fast indeed.

PETER: And so have I.

MARTHA: And I. Often. He was so light to carry!

MRS. CRATCHIT: Like as if there was little of him in this world for he'd begun already to leave for that other. And his father loved him such that it was no trouble, no trouble at all to lift him up.

And there is your father at the bedside carrying now a heavy load that slows him, as we all will do.

MARTHA: He was so light to carry!

Bob:	(*rejoining the family*) We'll go on Sundays. We'll lay him by the church and Sundays each will go to walk beside him. It will do us good to see how green a place it is. And we'll see it often. I promised him I'd always go a'walking with him. And we always will. My little child! My little child!
Martha:	You shall always be sad now, Papa. As will we all.
Bob:	The first of our little fellowship has parted. And we shall carry that sadness with us always, but we shall also be happy, my dears. And for remembrance of Tiny Tim we shall remind ourselves to be less quarrelsome and to be gracious with one another each day. We shall be happy even as we carry our sadness with us. And our happiness shall make our burden light.

Everyone hugs and cries.

Bob:	I am so happy. I am so happy.

The bell tolls once.

Scrooge *stands beside* Tiny Tim's *bed and considers the body.*

Scrooge:	It cannot be. It's too cruel, Spirit. Too cruel!

The Cratchit house fades away. Scrooge *and* Yet to Come *are alone in shadowy limbo. The Spirit points.*

Scrooge:	No. No. I won't go any further. You conjure these phantoms to torment me! But why? If you had any power to heal then the child would live. But you don't, do you! If you want to show me something. Show me that!

SCENE 8

YET TO COME *spreads its arms like black wings as the scene changes to a home where* MRS. MCCAWBER *is pacing anxiously.*

MR. MCCAWBER *enters.*

MRS. MCCAWBER: What took you so long and what did he say? Is it good—or bad?

MR. MCCAWBER: It's ... Ah ...

MRS. MCCAWBER: Speak up! Don't just stand there like a fool upon a gallows. Has something turned up or not? Is it good news or bad?

MR. MCCAWBER: Bad?

MRS. MCCAWBER: Then we are ruined. There's nothing for it.

MR. MCCAWBER: Emma ...

MRS. MCCAWBER: We are destitute and we'll be off to debtor's prison at Marshalsea in the week.

MR. MCCAWBER: Apple ...

MRS. McCAWBER: We're packing already, ain't we? But I always said it and I say it now: I never will abandon you, Mr. McCawber.

MR. McCAWBER: Dear . . .

MRS. McCAWBER: I never will.

MR. McCAWBER: Emma. Wait, dear. There is hope yet.

MRS. McCAWBER: Hope? Has he relented then? Nothing is past hope, if such a miracle has happened.

MR. McCAWBER: He is past relenting.

MRS. McCAWBER: What then?

MR. McCAWBER: He is, well, in short, my dear, in the very shortest . . . terms . . . well . . . he is . . . ah . . . dead.

MRS. McCAWBER: Oh!

MR. McCAWBER *and* MRS. McCAWBER *look at one another both frowning and smiling and unsure of how to react.*

BOTH: Merry Christmas!

MRS. McCAWBER: The Lord forgive me, it's unChristian of me, I'm sure, and I'm a sinner sure as I am a soft heart, but bless him for it. And bless us.

MR. McCAWBER: (*smiling*) Then God forgive us both! It's the most awful wonderful thing!

They bounce with joy.

SCROOGE: He's indebted to half the city! Even if he's dodged one of his accounts he won't dodge mine.

MR. MCCAWBER: We may sleep tonight with light hearts, Emma!
          At long last, something has turned up!

MRS. MCCAWBER: Merry Christmas, Mr. McCawber.

MR. MCCAWBER: Merry Christmas, my sweet apple.

SCROOGE: No. No. No. You are too cruel, Spirit. Surely
             there is on the earth someone who can show
             tenderness upon the death of another. Show it
             to me, now, I beg you. I beg you. Or that dark
             bedchamber and the form lying cold within it
             will forever haunt me.

SCENE 9

YET TO COME *points and* SCROOGE *grovels and obeys. They arrive at* BOB'*s house where all the joy from the last visit is gone and a pall of sadness hangs over all the scene.*

MARTHA: Will he be all right, papa?

BOB: We can but pray, my dear. Come, everyone. Let's put on our better faces for the doctor. His work is grim enough and we should not add to his burdens.

The family wipe their eyes and try to be cheerful as the DOCTOR *enters.*

MRS. CRATCHIT: Doctor! Does it go ill with him?

The DOCTOR *sighs and frowns.*

DOCTOR: Perhaps if I'd been here sooner. Perhaps if he'd had a treatment a year ago, or two . . . I am sorry.

The children cry. BOB *is stunned in silence. The* DOCTOR *packs his bag and begins to exit.*

MRS. CRATCHIT: (*through tears*) We would have sent for you before, but we have had so little . . . this is all that's left.

MRS. CRATCHIT *offers the doctor a handful of coins.*

DOCTOR: Keep what you have. You will need it more than I.

DOCTOR *exits.* MRS. CRATCHIT *tries to comfort* BOB, *but he backs away and shuffles slowly into* TINY TIM'S *room. The boy lies dead upon the bed with the sheet pulled over him, just as the previous bed and body shown to* SCROOGE. *This bed however is surrounded by toys and beloved things and is showered in golden light.* BOB *sits next to his son and cries.*

MARTHA: Is Tiny Tim gone, mama?

MRS. CRATCHIT *nods.*

PETER: Will papa be all right. Why does he move so slowly?

MRS. CRATCHIT: I have known him walk with . . . I have known him walk with Tiny Tim upon his shoulder very fast indeed.

PETER: And so have I.

MARTHA: And I. Often. He was so light to carry!

MRS. CRATCHIT: Like as if there was little of him in this world for he'd begun already to leave for that other. And his father loved him such that it was no trouble, no trouble at all to lift him up.

And there is your father at the bedside carrying now a heavy load that slows him, as we all will do.

MARTHA: He was so light to carry!

BOB: (*rejoining the family*) We'll go on Sundays. We'll
              lay him by the church and Sundays each will go
              to walk beside him. It will do us good to see how
              green a place it is. And we'll see it often. I prom-
              ised him I'd always go a'walking with him. And
              we always will. My little child! My little child!

MARTHA: You shall always be sad now, Papa. As will we all.

BOB: The first of our little fellowship has parted. And
              we shall carry that sadness with us always, but we
              shall also be happy, my dears. And for remem-
              brance of Tiny Tim we shall remind ourselves
              to be less quarrelsome and to be gracious with
              one another each day. We shall be happy even as
              we carry our sadness with us. And our happiness
              shall make our burden light.

Everyone hugs and cries.

BOB: I am so happy. I am so happy.

The bell tolls once.

SCROOGE *stands beside* TINY TIM's *bed and considers the body.*

SCROOGE: It cannot be. It's too cruel, Spirit. Too cruel!

The Cratchit house fades away. SCROOGE *and* YET TO COME *are
alone in shadowy limbo. The Spirit points.*

SCROOGE: No. No. I won't go any further. You conjure
              these phantoms to torment me! But why? If you
              had any power to heal then the child would live.
              But you don't, do you! If you want to show me
              something. Show me that!

YET TO COME *points emphatically. A spectral wind swallows up the stage. Lightning flashes. The spirit grows immense and terrible.* SCROOGE *hides his eyes.*

SCENE 10

The bell tolls again.

SCROOGE: Where are we? Is this it? What is this place?

SPIRIT 1 (LEAD): Look here upon the empty churchyard. Look here, the wretched name at last to learn. The man who lay upon the barren bed ...

SPIRIT 3:   ... now lies within the tomb.

SPIRIT 1 (LEAD): A worthy place. Walled in by cold stone.

SPIRIT 2:   Overrun by grass and weeds ...

SPIRIT 4:   ... the growth of a garden's death, not life.

SPIRIT 1 (LEAD): A graveyard fattened by its appetite. And all choked up with too much burying.

ALL: A worthy place!

YET TO COME *advances upon a mausoleum and points. It's doorway looms.*

Spirit 1 (Lead): And herein lies the man. A banker, a miser, a jealous counter of coin.

Spirit 4:   A man eaten away with usury and corruption, soaked in greed, a wanton acolyte before the altar of avarice.

Spirit 2:   A dead man?

Spirit 1 (Lead): Yes, dead.

Spirit 4:   Entirely dead?

Spirit 1 (Lead): Completely dead. There is no doubt whatsoever about *that*.

Spirit 3:   The register of his burial was signed by . . .

Spirit 1 (Lead): The clergyman.

Spirit 4:   The clerk.

Spirit 3:   The undertaker.

Spirit 4:   But are we *sure* he was . . .

All: (*turning to look at* Scrooge) Dead as a doornail!

Spirit 3:   (*whispering*) Read the name.

Spirit 4:   (*whispering*) Read the name.

Spirit 1 (Lead): *(flatly) Read the name.*

Scrooge: No! No! Take me away from this dread place!

All: Read the name!

Yet to Come *hovers beside the mausoleum door and raps his stave upon it. The spirits swirl around* Scrooge. *As he shrinks from them he is herded to the foot of the door.*

SCROOGE: Please. Please. Answer me one question. Are these shadows of things that will be, or are they only shadows of things that may be?

YET TO COME *is inexorable, pointing.*

SPIRIT 3: (*whispering*) What is hidden cannot heal.

SPIRIT 1 (LEAD): What is hidden cannot heal.

SPIRIT 2: (*whispering*) Read the name.

SPIRIT 1 (LEAD): (*whispering*) Read the name.

The COMPANY *of spirits slowly drag out chains and attach them to* SCROOGE, *binding him in their great weight.*

SCROOGE: Men's courses may foreshadow certain ends, but if those courses be departed from, the ends will change. Please, Spirit! Say it is so!

YET TO COME, *unrelenting, points ever to the stone.*

ALL: (*harsh whisper*) READ THE NAME.

SCROOGE GESTURES, *extending his arms toward the stone, as if to push it away. He* GESTURES *to* YET TO COME *to push it away. He* GESTURES *all around him.*

SCROOGE *turns to look and falls to his knees wailing and sobbing.*

Above the mausoleum door a series of letters is slowly illuminated: EBENEZER SCROOGE.

The door of the mausoleum creaks open. THE BOY *emerges silhouetted in ghastly light.*

The bell tolls, tolls, tolls.

The chains drag Scrooge *slowly toward the ghastly light of the grave/doorway.*

Scrooge *stretches his hand out to the* Boy, Gesturing *palm out to push him away, but then turning palm up for the first time.*

Scrooge: Help me.

The Boy *turns and walks coldly back into the mausoleum. The* Company *follow, dragging* Scrooge *in chains into the grave.*

Scrooge: I will honor Christmas in my heart and keep it all the year long. I will live in the Past, the Present, and the Future! The threefold-Spirit shall strive within me and be with me always. I swear it, Jacob! I swear it!

The mausoleum door slams shut. Darkness.

Spirit 4:   (*whispered*) What happened?

Spirit 2:   Did it work?

Spirit 3:   Did it work?

Spirit 1 (Lead) *looks around suspiciously as the others step back into shadow. He peers at the mausoleum in silence, then turns to the audience with a smirk on his face and exits.*

SCENE 11

The scene is again SCROOGE's *bedroom. The clock finishes its toll. The sun is up.* SCROOGE *bolts upright in bed.*

SCROOGE: I'm back. I'm here. Was it real? It all happened, didn't it? And now I'm here. I'm alive. And it's now, not then, or when, or there, it's here.

SCROOGE *slowly begins to brighten.*

SCROOGE: What do I do? I . . . I don't know what to do. I'm . . . I'm . . . I think I'm . . . merry. I am. I'm as merry as a schoolboy. It's an odd giddy feeling . . . here . . . and here . . . and how remarkable . . . even here! I am as giddy as a drunken man! What day is it? How long have I been among those Spirits? A day? A night? A year? I don't know anything. I'm a baby! I'm new. I'm old. I'm . . . me. I'm something else. I don't know what I am!

SCROOGE *is interrupted in his discovery by the ringing of church bells, but not the ominous toll of the night's adventures, rather the great melodic pealing of all the bells in the city crying out in celebration.*

SCROOGE *runs to the window and throws it open. He sees an* URCHIN *in the street.*

SCROOGE: You there! What's today?

URCHIN: You talkin' to me?

SCROOGE: What's today, I say?

URCHIN: Today? Why, it's Christmas Day.

SCROOGE: The Spirits have done it all in one night! They can do anything they like. Of course they can. Of course they can. Do you know the Poulterer's, in the next street, at the corner?

URCHIN: Course I do!

SCROOGE: What an intelligent boy! A remarkable boy! Do you know whether they've sold the prize turkey that was hanging up there? Not the little prize turkey: the BIG one?

URCHIN: What, the one as big as me?

SCROOGE: Yes, my boy! The one as big as you! What a delightful boy!

              Go and buy it. And tell them to bring it here so that I may give them directions of where to take it. Come back with the man and I'll give you a shilling. Come back with him in less than five minutes and I'll give you half-a-crown!

URCHIN: Blimey!

The URCHIN *runs off happily.*

SCROOGE: (*writing an address on a piece of paper*) He won't
                know who sent it, and oh, I wish I could see the
                look on his face when... Where am I? Hat. Coat.
                Cane. Cane? No cane. Scarf perhaps? What does
                it matter.

SCROOGE *dresses and walks to the door where he meets the* URCHIN
along with the TURKEY MAN *who is burdened with a gargantuan
bird.*

SCROOGE *flips the* URCHIN *a coin.*

SCROOGE: A half-crown for you, my boy!

URCHIN: Thank you, sir! Merry Christmas!

SCROOGE: Mer—Merry Christmas to you! Here you are,
                sir, see this fat bird off to this address double-
                quick and here's extra for your trouble.

The TURKEY MAN *runs off with the turkey.* SCROOGE *takes up his
cane and closes his door behind him. He comes face to face with his
knocker. He kisses it.*

SCROOGE: Bless you, Jacob, and your door-knocker too.
                I shall love it as long as I live! It's a wonderful
                knocker!

SCENE 12

SCROOGE *walks to the office, encountering folks along the way and wishing them all a Merry Christmas.*

SPIRIT 1 (LEAD): Good morning, sir! A merry Christmas to you!

SCROOGE: (*moved*) To me? Do you mean it? Thank you! And . . . merrier still to you!

SCROOGE *passes the* COLLECTORS *on the street. They frown at him and step wide.* SCROOGE *stops, turns and calls to them.*

SCROOGE: Sir! You there! Have you raised your collection for the Poor?

COLLECTOR 1: Mr. Scrooge?

SCROOGE: Yes. That is my name, and I have an offer for you.

The COLLECTOR *is suspicious as* SCROOGE *whispers in his ear.*

COLLECTOR 1: My dear Mr. Scrooge, are you serious?

SCROOGE: I'm more than serious. I am . . . persuaded. And you will accept not a farthing less. A great many back-payments are included in that number, I assure you. Take this as a deposit and visit me in my office as soon as you are able.

SCROOGE *hands the* COLLECTOR *a heavy coinpurse.*

COLLECTOR 2: My dear sir, I don't know what to say to such generos—

SCROOGE: Don't say anything at all. Come and see me and I shall make good on it. And . . . and I think perhaps it would do me good to hear your views on what's in need and who and how--and how we might achieve some greater end.

COLLECTOR 1: I would enjoy that, Mr. Scrooge. Very much, I would. I will!

SCROOGE: I am much obliged to you. I thank you fifty times, sir, and I beg your pardon seventy times seven. Bless you! Bless you both!

SPIRIT 3: I . . . I think he means it too!

SPIRIT 1 (LEAD): I heard he went to church.

SPIRIT 3: Did he just pat that child on the head?

SPIRIT 2: What's he doing now? He's never talked to a beggar in his long life and . . .

SCROOGE *drops coins into a* BEGGAR's *cup.*

SPIRIT 4: Did he just . . .

SPIRIT 1 (LEAD): Now he's looking into the kitchens of houses, and up to the windows, and . . . what's that?

SPIRIT 2: He's . . . smiling.

SCROOGE: I never dreamed that a mere walk in the city could give so much joy. And I know just where to go next.

SCROOGE *knocks on* FRED'*s door.*

FRED: Uncle?

SCROOGE: Fred!

FRED: Why bless my soul!

SCROOGE: It is I. Your uncle Scrooge. I have come to tell you that I shall join you for dinner. If the offer stands, that is.

FRED: Of course! You're welcome! You're always welcome!

CLARA: Hello, uncle. Is everything all right?

SCROOGE: All right? Nothing wrong whatever. It's as good as it can be, and I'm sure dinner itself will be even better. Perhaps we can even play games!

CLARA: Why yes, I suppose we could.

SCROOGE: Will you allow me to bring something to add to the feast?

FRED: Bring yourself, uncle, and nothing more!

SCROOGE: Then I shall look forward to it. But before I go, may I give you something?

FRED: Give me something?

SCROOGE: (*handing over a small box*) Merry Christmas, Fred.

FRED *opens the box and removes* FAN'*s locket.*

SCROOGE: It was your mother's. It has only ever hung upon a beloved breast and, well, Fred, you should have it. Perhaps you will find some good use for it.

CLARA: What is it? It's lovely.

FRED *hangs it about his wife's neck.*

SCROOGE: Yes. Yes, that's just right. Just as it should be. I do miss your mother, Fred, and I hope you'll allow me to tell you all about her at dinner.

FRED: (*embracing* SCROOGE) Thank you, uncle. Thank you.

SCROOGE: I'll see you all at dinner. I have work to do.

All are amazed as SCROOGE *exits.*

SCROOGE: And now, let us see if that prize turkey has got itself delivered.

SCROOGE *looks in the window at the Cratchit family as the* TURKEY-MAN *knocks.*

BOB: Hallo? Are you lost, sir.

TURKEY-MAN: It's for Cratchits, sir!

BOB: What is?

TURKEY-MAN: This beast of a bird, sir. If you're a Cratchit say so now and let me in or I'll drop this turkey on the street.

MRS. CRATCHIT: Well come in, come in. But who have you come from? We haven't sent for such a bird as that, I'm sure!

TURKEY-MAN: I ain't to say, miss. But I'll thank you to take it from me and make a merry Christmas of it.

The TURKEY-MAN *plops the bird onto the table and departs.*

BOB: But who can—

MRS. CRATCHIT: Never you mind, Bob Cratchit. There's a mighty bird and there's an oven to cook it. Bless my soul.

PETER: I can't even lift it! Help me carry it, Martha!

MRS. CRATCHIT: That's it. Into the kitchen!

TINY TIM: It's bigger than I am, mother!

MRS. CRATCHIT: Bless me, it's bigger than us both!

As the children carry the turkey away, Bob looks around in wonder. SCROOGE, *peeking through the window, giggles with joy.* SCROOGE *knocks at the door and* BOB *answers.*

BOB: Mr. Scrooge. Why, hello. I mean . . . good morning. I mean . . . Merry—

SCROOGE: (*sternly*) Bob Cratchit.

BOB: I'm sorry, sir. But you said I could have the day, sir. It's but once a year, I said, and you said, or I thought you said, sir—

SCROOGE: I'll tell you what, Bob Cratchit. I'm not going to stand for this sort of thing.

BOB: I'm sorry, sir.

MRS. CRATCHIT: Robert. Don't.

SCROOGE: And therefore...

MRS. CRATCHIT: Mr. Scrooge, please.

SCROOGE: Therefore I am raising your salary.

MRS. CRATCHIT: What?

BOB: I beg you sir, don't mock me.

SCROOGE: Mock you? I mean no mockery. I mean you a
                 merry Christmas!

BOB: What?

SCROOGE: I mean all the merriment you can muster. I'll see
                 your cups filled to the brim and slopping over
                 for it's such a day as Christmas, Bob. And your
                 plates too. Get that prize turkey in the oven,
                 Mrs. Cratchit.

MRS. CRATCHIT: Was that your doing? I don't believe—

SCROOGE: And that's not all. First the turkey, second the
                 salary, and then we'll discuss all your affairs this
                 afternoon over a bowl of smoking bishop! Stoke
                 the fires, Bob. Order another coal-scuttle. And
                 send for that doctor.

BOB: The doctor, sir?

SCROOGE: Tell him to attend your Tiny Tim and get him
                 whatever medicines money can buy. Send me
                 the bill. I'm good for it if I'm good for anything,
                 Bob.

BOB: I don't know what to say.

SCROOGE: Say nothing at all, my good man. Say you'll keep
                Christmas today, and tomorrow we'll discuss
                your future.

MRS. CRATCHIT: Thank you, Mr. Scrooge. Bless you, sir.

SCENE 13

SCROOGE *shakes* BOB's *hand and retreats into the street. He sees the* BOY *who haunted him upon his stoop. The* BOY *and* SCROOGE *face one another across the distance as carols begin.*

SCROOGE: (*softly*) I see you now, my boy. And I shall hide from you no longer. Merry Christmas.

SCROOGE *offers his outstretched hands to the* BOY. *They embrace. They spin around and the* BOY *is gone, only* SCROOGE *remains.*

SPIRIT 3:   That's it!

SPIRIT 2:   Is it done?

SPIRIT 4:   They've done it, haven't they?

SPIRIT 1 (LEAD): Look at him. He's just as he ought to be. He's all himself.

SPIRIT 3:   All at once.

SPIRIT 4:   And all the time.

SPIRIT 3:   Past and Present ...

SPIRIT 4:   And ... Yet to Come?

SCROOGE *looks around and accosts a* LONDONER.

SCROOGE: You, sir. Can you paint? I have a job for you and
                  I'll pay you a crown if it's done quick.

SCROOGE *and the* LONDONER *confer and* SCROOGE *points up at
the counting house sign. The* LONDONER *runs off as the scene continues.*

SPIRIT 1 (LEAD): Yes, and "yet to come." In the time to come there
                  followed a string of golden days stretching for
                  more years than anyone ever dared hope. And
                  at their culmination a gentle ending worthy of a
                  tale or a song.

SPIRIT 4:   Someone should write it down!

The LONDONER *returns with paint and brush, the counting house
sign is lowered as he begins to work.*

SCROOGE: There's a good man! Now, look here. Make it like
                  this.

SPIRIT 1 (LEAD): For Scrooge was better than his word.

SPIRIT 4:   He did it all—the cheer, the charity, the good
                  will.

SPIRIT 1 (LEAD): And infinitely more.

SCROOGE: Yes! That's just it. No. Wait. The other way
                  around, I think.

SPIRIT 1 (LEAD): He set himself about the business of human-
                  kind.

SPIRIT 3:   He invested himself in it night and day.

SPIRIT 1 (LEAD): And all who crossed his path found their spirits profited in his presence.

SCROOGE: Excellent! Perfect. Raise it up! UP!

SPIRIT 1 (LEAD): The old Scrooge is gone, a man amended, a new creation. And all who know him agree.

The LONDONER *hoists up the sign and it reads: "Cratchit & Scrooge"*

Everyone applauds.

SCROOGE *is joined by the Cratchit family. He extends his arms to them. They embrace.*

SPIRIT 1 (LEAD): And to Tiny Tim ...

SPIRIT 3:   ... who did not die ...

SPIRIT 1 (LEAD): ... he is a second father.

SCROOGE *kneels down as* TINY TIM *enters.*

SPIRIT 2:   He is as good a friend ...

SPIRIT 3:   ... and as good a man ...

SPIRIT 1 (LEAD): ... as the good old city has ever known.

SPIRIT 2:   Or any other good old city ...

SPIRIT 1 (LEAD): ... in the good old world.

SCROOGE: Everyone come here. Gather round. I'll tell you a story.

TINY TIM: A story? What kind?

SCROOGE: Did you ever hear of Jacob Marley, my boy? Yes?
                Well let me tell you again. To begin with, Marley
                was . . .

BOB: Not this one again.

SCROOGE: Yes, this one. Again. Because it's true, it's all true,
                and I'll tell you just how it all happened. Come
                close.

*SCROOGE's voice is drowned out in laughter and conversation. The
family gather around him as* SCROOGE *begins to act out the tale of
Marley's haunting.*

SPIRIT 1 (LEAD): It will be said of him ever after . . .

SPIRIT 3:   *. . . that he hid himself away no longer.*

SCROOGE: And then you stood up tall, and you raised your
                cup into the air, and you said . . .

TINY TIM: God bless us, every one!

SPIRIT 1 (LEAD): And he kept Christmas well.

SCROOGE: Yes. Yes, just exactly that. Well done, old boy.

                Look at you. Aren't you lovely. Aren't you *all*
                lovely.

The company of spirits each acknowledge SCROOGE *with a bow or
a hat-tip or a wave and step back into shadow one by one until only*
SCROOGE *and* TINY TIM *remain.*

SCROOGE: God bless us: them, you, me, all of us, each and
                every one.

THE END

RABBIT ROOM
THEATRE

A Christmas Carol
by Charles Dickens

PREFACE

I HAVE endeavoured in this Ghostly little book, to raise the Ghost of an Idea, which shall not put my readers out of humour with themselves, with each other, with the season, or with me. May it haunt their houses pleasantly, and no one wish to lay it.

Their faithful Friend and Servant,
C. D.
December, 1843.

STAVE I: MARLEY'S GHOST

MARLEY was dead: to begin with. There is no doubt whatever about that. The register of his burial was signed by the clergyman, the clerk, the undertaker, and the chief mourner. Scrooge signed it: and Scrooge's name was good upon 'Change, for anything he chose to put his hand to. Old Marley was as dead as a door-nail.

Mind! I don't mean to say that I know, of my own knowledge, what there is particularly dead about a door-nail. I might have been inclined, myself, to regard a coffin-nail as the deadest piece of ironmongery in the trade. But the wisdom of our ancestors is in the simile; and my unhallowed hands shall not disturb it, or the Country's done for. You will therefore permit me to repeat, emphatically, that Marley was as dead as a door-nail.

Scrooge knew he was dead? Of course he did. How could it be otherwise? Scrooge and he were partners for I don't know how many years. Scrooge was his sole executor, his sole administrator, his sole assign, his sole residuary legatee, his sole friend, and sole mourner. And even Scrooge was not so dreadfully cut up by the sad event, but that he was an excellent man of business on the very day of the funeral, and solemnised it with an undoubted bargain.

The mention of Marley's funeral brings me back to the point I started from. There is no doubt that Marley was dead. This must be distinctly understood, or nothing wonderful can come of the story I am going to relate. If we were not perfectly convinced that Hamlet's Father died before the play began, there would be nothing more remarkable in his taking a stroll at night, in an easterly wind, upon his own ramparts, than there would be in any other middle-aged gentleman rashly turning out after dark in a breezy spot–say Saint Paul's Churchyard for instance– literally to astonish his son's weak mind.

Scrooge never painted out Old Marley's name. There it stood, years afterwards, above the warehouse door: Scrooge and Marley. The firm was known as Scrooge and Marley. Sometimes people new to the business called Scrooge Scrooge, and sometimes Marley, but he answered to both names. It was all the same to him.

Oh! But he was a tight-fisted hand at the grind-stone, Scrooge! a squeezing, wrenching, grasping, scraping, clutching, covetous, old sinner! Hard and sharp as flint, from which no steel had ever struck out generous fire; secret, and self-contained, and solitary as an oyster. The cold within him froze his old features, nipped his pointed nose, shrivelled his cheek, stiffened his gait; made his eyes red, his thin lips blue; and spoke out shrewdly in his grating voice. A frosty rime was on his head, and on his eyebrows, and his wiry chin. He carried his own low temperature always about with him; he iced his office in the dog-days; and didn't thaw it one degree at Christmas.

External heat and cold had little influence on Scrooge. No warmth could warm, no wintry weather chill him. No wind that blew was bitterer than he, no falling snow was more intent upon its purpose, no pelting rain less open to entreaty. Foul weather didn't know where to have him. The heaviest rain, and snow, and hail, and sleet, could boast of the advantage over him in only one respect. They often "came down" handsomely, and Scrooge never did.

Nobody ever stopped him in the street to say, with gladsome looks, "My dear Scrooge, how are you? When will you come to see me?" No beggars implored him to bestow a trifle, no children asked him what it was o'clock, no man or woman ever once in all his life inquired the way to such and such a place, of Scrooge. Even the blind men's dogs appeared to know him; and when they saw him coming on, would tug their owners into doorways and up courts; and then would wag their tails as though they said, "No eye at all is better than an evil eye, dark master!"

But what did Scrooge care! It was the very thing he liked. To edge his way along the crowded paths of life, warning all human sympathy to keep its distance, was what the knowing ones call "nuts" to Scrooge.

Once upon a time—of all the good days in the year, on Christmas Eve—old Scrooge sat busy in his counting-house. It was cold, bleak, biting weather: foggy withal: and he could hear the people in the court outside, go wheezing up and down, beating their hands upon their breasts, and stamping their feet upon the pavement stones to warm them. The city clocks had only just gone three, but it was quite dark already–it had not been light all day–and candles were flaring in the windows of the neighbouring offices, like ruddy smears upon the palpable brown air. The fog came pouring in at every chink and keyhole, and was so dense without, that although the court was of the narrowest, the houses opposite were mere phantoms. To see the dingy cloud come drooping down, obscuring everything, one might have thought that Nature lived hard by, and was brewing on a large scale.

The door of Scrooge's counting-house was open that he might keep his eye upon his clerk, who in a dismal little cell beyond, a sort of tank, was copying letters. Scrooge had a very small fire, but the clerk's fire was so very much smaller that it looked like one coal. But he couldn't replenish it, for Scrooge kept the coal-box in his own room; and so surely as the clerk came in with the shovel, the master predicted that it would be necessary for them to part. Wherefore the clerk put on his white comforter, and tried to warm himself at the candle; in which effort, not being a man of a strong imagination, he failed.

"A merry Christmas, uncle! God save you!" cried a cheerful voice. It was the voice of Scrooge's nephew, who came upon him so quickly that this was the first intimation he had of his approach.

"Bah!" said Scrooge, "Humbug!"

He had so heated himself with rapid walking in the fog and frost, this nephew of Scrooge's, that he was all in a glow; his face was ruddy and handsome; his eyes sparkled, and his breath smoked again.

"Christmas a humbug, uncle!" said Scrooge's nephew. "You don't mean that, I am sure?"

"I do," said Scrooge. "Merry Christmas! What right have you to be merry? What reason have you to be merry? You're poor enough."

"Come, then," returned the nephew gaily. "What right have you to be dismal? What reason have you to be morose? You're rich enough."

Scrooge having no better answer ready on the spur of the moment, said, "Bah!" again; and followed it up with "Humbug."

"Don't be cross, uncle!" said the nephew.

"What else can I be," returned the uncle, "when I live in such a world of fools as this? Merry Christmas! Out upon merry Christmas! What's Christmas time to you but a time for paying bills without money; a time for finding yourself a year older, but not an hour richer; a time for balancing your books and having every item in 'em through a round dozen of months presented dead against you? If I could work my will," said Scrooge indignantly, "every idiot who goes about with 'Merry Christmas' on his lips, should be boiled with his own pudding, and buried with a stake of holly through his heart. He should!"

"Uncle!" pleaded the nephew.

"Nephew!" returned the uncle sternly, "keep Christmas in your own way, and let me keep it in mine."

"Keep it!" repeated Scrooge's nephew. "But you don't keep it."

"Let me leave it alone, then," said Scrooge. "Much good may it do you! Much good it has ever done you!"

"There are many things from which I might have derived good, by which I have not profited, I dare say," returned the nephew. "Christmas among the rest. But I am sure I have always thought of Christmas time, when it has come round–apart from the veneration due to its sacred name and origin, if anything belonging to it can be apart from that–as a good time; a kind, forgiving, charitable, pleasant time; the only time I know of, in the long calendar of the year, when men and women seem by one consent to open their shut-up hearts freely, and to think of people below them as if they really were fellow-passengers to the grave, and not another race of creatures bound on other journeys. And therefore, uncle, though it has never put a scrap of gold or silver in my pocket, I believe that it has done me good, and will do me good; and I say, God bless it!"

The clerk in the Tank involuntarily applauded. Becoming immediately sensible of the impropriety, he poked the fire, and extinguished the last frail spark for ever.

"Let me hear another sound from you," said Scrooge, "and you'll keep your Christmas by losing your situation! You're quite a powerful speaker, sir," he added, turning to his nephew. "I wonder you don't go into Parliament."

"Don't be angry, uncle. Come! Dine with us to-morrow."

Scrooge said that he would see him–yes, indeed he did. He went the whole length of the expression, and said that he would see him in that extremity first.

"But why?" cried Scrooge's nephew. "Why?"

"Why did you get married?" said Scrooge.

"Because I fell in love."

"Because you fell in love!" growled Scrooge, as if that were the only one thing in the world more ridiculous than a merry Christmas. "Good afternoon!"

"Nay, uncle, but you never came to see me before that happened. Why give it as a reason for not coming now?"

"Good afternoon," said Scrooge.

"I want nothing from you; I ask nothing of you; why cannot we be friends?"

"Good afternoon," said Scrooge.

"I am sorry, with all my heart, to find you so resolute. We have never had any quarrel, to which I have been a party. But I have made the trial in homage to Christmas, and I'll keep my Christmas humour to the last. So A Merry Christmas, uncle!"

"Good afternoon!" said Scrooge.

"And A Happy New Year!"

"Good afternoon!" said Scrooge.

His nephew left the room without an angry word, notwithstanding. He stopped at the outer door to bestow the greetings of the season on the clerk, who, cold as he was, was warmer than Scrooge; for he returned them cordially.

"There's another fellow," muttered Scrooge; who overheard him: "my clerk, with fifteen shillings a week, and a wife and family, talking about a merry Christmas. I'll retire to Bedlam."

This lunatic, in letting Scrooge's nephew out, had let two other people in. They were portly gentlemen, pleasant to behold, and now stood, with their hats off, in Scrooge's office. They had books and papers in their hands, and bowed to him.

"Scrooge and Marley's, I believe," said one of the gentlemen, referring to his list. "Have I the pleasure of addressing Mr. Scrooge, or Mr. Marley?"

"Mr. Marley has been dead these seven years," Scrooge replied. "He died seven years ago, this very night."

"We have no doubt his liberality is well represented by his surviving partner," said the gentleman, presenting his credentials.

It certainly was; for they had been two kindred spirits. At the ominous word "liberality," Scrooge frowned, and shook his head, and handed the credentials back.

"At this festive season of the year, Mr. Scrooge," said the gentleman, taking up a pen, "it is more than usually desirable that we should make some slight provision for the Poor and destitute, who suffer greatly at the present time. Many thousands are in want of common necessaries; hundreds of thousands are in want of common comforts, sir."

"Are there no prisons?" asked Scrooge.

"Plenty of prisons," said the gentleman, laying down the pen again.

"And the Union workhouses?" demanded Scrooge. "Are they still in operation?"

"They are. Still," returned the gentleman, "I wish I could say they were not."

"The Treadmill and the Poor Law are in full vigour, then?" said Scrooge.

"Both very busy, sir."

"Oh! I was afraid, from what you said at first, that something had occurred to stop them in their useful course," said Scrooge. "I'm very glad to hear it."

"Under the impression that they scarcely furnish Christian cheer of mind or body to the multitude," returned the gentleman, "a few of us are endeavouring to raise a fund to buy the Poor some meat and drink, and means of warmth. We choose this time, because it is a time, of all others, when Want is keenly felt, and Abundance rejoices. What shall I put you down for?"

"Nothing!" Scrooge replied.

"You wish to be anonymous?"

"I wish to be left alone," said Scrooge. "Since you ask me what I wish, gentlemen, that is my answer. I don't make merry myself at Christmas and I can't afford to make idle people merry. I help to support the establishments I have mentioned—they cost enough; and those who are badly off must go there."

"Many can't go there; and many would rather die."

"If they would rather die," said Scrooge, "they had better do it, and decrease the surplus population. Besides—excuse me—I don't know that."

"But you might know it," observed the gentleman.

"It's not my business," Scrooge returned. "It's enough for a man to understand his own business, and not to interfere with other people's. Mine occupies me constantly. Good afternoon, gentlemen!"

Seeing clearly that it would be useless to pursue their point, the gentlemen withdrew. Scrooge resumed his labours with an improved opinion of himself, and in a more facetious temper than was usual with him.

Meanwhile the fog and darkness thickened so, that people ran about with flaring links, proffering their services to go before horses in carriages, and conduct them on their way. The ancient tower of a church, whose gruff old bell was always peeping slily down at Scrooge out of a Gothic window in the wall, became invisible, and struck the hours and quarters in the clouds, with tremulous vibrations afterwards as if its teeth were chattering in its frozen head up there. The cold became intense. In the main street, at the corner of the court, some labourers were repairing the gas-pipes, and had lighted a great fire in a brazier, round which a party of ragged men and boys were gathered: warming their hands and winking their eyes before the blaze in rapture. The water-plug being left in solitude, its overflowings sullenly congealed, and turned to misanthropic ice. The brightness of the shops where holly sprigs and berries crackled in the lamp heat of the windows, made pale faces ruddy as they passed. Poulterers' and grocers' trades became a splendid joke: a glorious pageant, with which it was next to impossible to believe that such dull principles as bargain and sale had anything to do. The Lord Mayor, in the stronghold of the mighty Mansion House, gave orders to his fifty cooks and butlers to keep Christmas as a Lord Mayor's household should; and even the little tailor, whom he had fined five shillings on the previous Monday for being drunk and bloodthirsty in the streets, stirred up to-morrow's pudding in his garret, while his lean wife and the baby sallied out to buy the beef.

Foggier yet, and colder. Piercing, searching, biting cold. If the good Saint Dunstan had but nipped the Evil Spirit's nose with a touch of such weather as that, instead of using his familiar weapons, then indeed he would have roared to lusty purpose. The owner of one scant young nose, gnawed and mumbled by the hungry cold as bones are gnawed by dogs, stooped down at Scrooge's keyhole to regale him with a Christmas carol: but at the first sound of

"God bless you, merry gentleman!

May nothing you dismay!"

Scrooge seized the ruler with such energy of action, that the singer fled in terror, leaving the keyhole to the fog and even more congenial frost.

At length the hour of shutting up the counting-house arrived. With an ill-will Scrooge dismounted from his stool, and tacitly admitted the fact to the expectant clerk in the Tank, who instantly snuffed his candle out, and put on his hat.

"You'll want all day to-morrow, I suppose?" said Scrooge.

"If quite convenient, sir."

"It's not convenient," said Scrooge, "and it's not fair. If I was to stop half-a-crown for it, you'd think yourself ill-used, I'll be bound?"

The clerk smiled faintly.

"And yet," said Scrooge, "you don't think me ill-used, when I pay a day's wages for no work."

The clerk observed that it was only once a year.

"A poor excuse for picking a man's pocket every twenty-fifth of December!" said Scrooge, buttoning his great-coat to the chin. "But I suppose you must have the whole day. Be here all the earlier next morning."

The clerk promised that he would; and Scrooge walked out with a growl. The office was closed in a twinkling, and the clerk, with the long ends of his white comforter dangling below his waist (for he boasted no great-coat), went down a slide on

Cornhill, at the end of a lane of boys, twenty times, in honour of its being Christmas Eve, and then ran home to Camden Town as hard as he could pelt, to play at blindman's-buff.

Scrooge took his melancholy dinner in his usual melancholy tavern; and having read all the newspapers, and beguiled the rest of the evening with his banker's-book, went home to bed. He lived in chambers which had once belonged to his deceased partner. They were a gloomy suite of rooms, in a lowering pile of building up a yard, where it had so little business to be, that one could scarcely help fancying it must have run there when it was a young house, playing at hide-and-seek with other houses, and forgotten the way out again. It was old enough now, and dreary enough, for nobody lived in it but Scrooge, the other rooms being all let out as offices. The yard was so dark that even Scrooge, who knew its every stone, was fain to grope with his hands. The fog and frost so hung about the black old gateway of the house, that it seemed as if the Genius of the Weather sat in mournful meditation on the threshold.

Now, it is a fact, that there was nothing at all particular about the knocker on the door, except that it was very large. It is also a fact, that Scrooge had seen it, night and morning, during his whole residence in that place; also that Scrooge had as little of what is called fancy about him as any man in the city of London, even including—which is a bold word—the corporation, aldermen, and livery. Let it also be borne in mind that Scrooge had not bestowed one thought on Marley, since his last mention of his seven years' dead partner that afternoon. And then let any man explain to me, if he can, how it happened that Scrooge, having his key in the lock of the door, saw in the knocker, without its undergoing any intermediate process of change—not a knocker, but Marley's face.

Marley's face. It was not in impenetrable shadow as the other objects in the yard were, but had a dismal light about it, like a bad lobster in a dark cellar. It was not angry or ferocious, but looked at Scrooge as Marley used to look: with ghostly spectacles turned up on its ghostly forehead. The hair was curiously stirred, as if by breath or hot air; and, though the eyes were wide open, they were perfectly motionless. That, and its livid colour, made it horrible; but its horror seemed to be in spite of the face and beyond its control, rather than a part of its own expression.

As Scrooge looked fixedly at this phenomenon, it was a knocker again.

To say that he was not startled, or that his blood was not conscious of a terrible sensation to which it had been a stranger from infancy, would be untrue. But he put his hand upon the key he had relinquished, turned it sturdily, walked in, and lighted his candle.

He did pause, with a moment's irresolution, before he shut the door; and he did look cautiously behind it first, as if he half expected to be terrified with the sight of Marley's pigtail sticking out into the hall. But there was nothing on the back of the door, except the screws and nuts that held the knocker on, so he said "Pooh, pooh!" and closed it with a bang.

The sound resounded through the house like thunder. Every room above, and every cask in the wine-merchant's cellars below, appeared to have a separate peal of echoes of its own. Scrooge was not a man to be frightened by echoes. He fastened the door, and walked across the hall, and up the stairs; slowly too: trimming his candle as he went.

You may talk vaguely about driving a coach-and-six up a good old flight of stairs, or through a bad young Act of Parliament; but I mean to say you might have got a hearse up that staircase, and taken it broadwise, with the splinter-bar towards the wall and the door towards the balustrades: and done it easy. There was plenty of width for that, and room to spare; which is perhaps the reason why Scrooge thought he saw a locomotive hearse going on before him in the gloom. Half-a-dozen gas-lamps out of the street wouldn't have lighted the entry too well, so you may suppose that it was pretty dark with Scrooge's dip.

Up Scrooge went, not caring a button for that. Darkness is cheap, and Scrooge liked it. But before he shut his heavy door, he walked through his rooms to see that all was right. He had just enough recollection of the face to desire to do that.

Sitting-room, bedroom, lumber-room. All as they should be. Nobody under the table, nobody under the sofa; a small fire in the grate; spoon and basin ready; and the little saucepan of gruel (Scrooge had a cold in his head) upon the hob. Nobody under the bed; nobody in the closet; nobody in his dressing-gown, which was hanging up in a suspicious attitude against the wall. Lumber-room as usual. Old fire-guard, old shoes, two fish-baskets, washing-stand on three legs, and a poker.

Quite satisfied, he closed his door, and locked himself in; double-locked himself in, which was not his custom. Thus secured against surprise, he took off his cravat; put on his dress-

ing-gown and slippers, and his nightcap; and sat down before
the fire to take his gruel.

It was a very low fire indeed; nothing on such a bitter night.
He was obliged to sit close to it, and brood over it, before he
could extract the least sensation of warmth from such a handful
of fuel. The fireplace was an old one, built by some Dutch
merchant long ago, and paved all round with quaint Dutch
tiles, designed to illustrate the Scriptures. There were Cains
and Abels, Pharaoh's daughters; Queens of Sheba, Angelic
messengers descending through the air on clouds like feath-
er-beds, Abrahams, Belshazzars, Apostles putting off to sea in
butter-boats, hundreds of figures to attract his thoughts; and
yet that face of Marley, seven years dead, came like the ancient
Prophet's rod, and swallowed up the whole. If each smooth tile
had been a blank at first, with power to shape some picture on
its surface from the disjointed fragments of his thoughts, there
would have been a copy of old Marley's head on every one.

"Humbug!" said Scrooge; and walked across the room.

After several turns, he sat down again. As he threw his
head back in the chair, his glance happened to rest upon a bell,
a disused bell, that hung in the room, and communicated for
some purpose now forgotten with a chamber in the highest
story of the building. It was with great astonishment, and with
a strange, inexplicable dread, that as he looked, he saw this bell
begin to swing. It swung so softly in the outset that it scarcely
made a sound; but soon it rang out loudly, and so did every bell
in the house.

This might have lasted half a minute, or a minute, but it
seemed an hour. The bells ceased as they had begun, together.

They were succeeded by a clanking noise, deep down below; as if some person were dragging a heavy chain over the casks in the wine-merchant's cellar. Scrooge then remembered to have heard that ghosts in haunted houses were described as dragging chains.

The cellar-door flew open with a booming sound, and then he heard the noise much louder, on the floors below; then coming up the stairs; then coming straight towards his door.

"It's humbug still!" said Scrooge. "I won't believe it."

His colour changed though, when, without a pause, it came on through the heavy door, and passed into the room before his eyes. Upon its coming in, the dying flame leaped up, as though it cried, "I know him; Marley's Ghost!" and fell again.

The same face: the very same. Marley in his pigtail, usual waistcoat, tights and boots; the tassels on the latter bristling, like his pigtail, and his coat-skirts, and the hair upon his head. The chain he drew was clasped about his middle. It was long, and wound about him like a tail; and it was made (for Scrooge observed it closely) of cash-boxes, keys, padlocks, ledgers, deeds, and heavy purses wrought in steel. His body was transparent; so that Scrooge, observing him, and looking through his waistcoat, could see the two buttons on his coat behind.

Scrooge had often heard it said that Marley had no bowels, but he had never believed it until now.

No, nor did he believe it even now. Though he looked the phantom through and through, and saw it standing before him; though he felt the chilling influence of its death-cold eyes; and marked the very texture of the folded kerchief bound about its head and chin, which wrapper he had not observed before; he was still incredulous, and fought against his senses.

"How now!" said Scrooge, caustic and cold as ever. "What do you want with me?"

"Much!"–Marley's voice, no doubt about it.

"Who are you?"

"Ask me who I was."

"Who were you then?" said Scrooge, raising his voice. "You're particular, for a shade." He was going to say "to a shade," but substituted this, as more appropriate.

"In life I was your partner, Jacob Marley."

"Can you–can you sit down?" asked Scrooge, looking doubtfully at him.

"I can."

"Do it, then."

Scrooge asked the question, because he didn't know whether a ghost so transparent might find himself in a condition to take a chair; and felt that in the event of its being impossible, it might involve the necessity of an embarrassing explanation. But the ghost sat down on the opposite side of the fireplace, as if he were quite used to it.

"You don't believe in me," observed the Ghost.

"I don't," said Scrooge.

"What evidence would you have of my reality beyond that of your senses?"

"I don't know," said Scrooge.

"Why do you doubt your senses?"

"Because," said Scrooge, "a little thing affects them. A slight disorder of the stomach makes them cheats. You may be an undigested bit of beef, a blot of mustard, a crumb of cheese, a fragment of an underdone potato. There's more of gravy than of grave about you, whatever you are!"

Scrooge was not much in the habit of cracking jokes, nor did he feel, in his heart, by any means waggish then. The truth is, that he tried to be smart, as a means of distracting his own attention, and keeping down his terror; for the spectre's voice disturbed the very marrow in his bones.

To sit, staring at those fixed glazed eyes, in silence for a moment, would play, Scrooge felt, the very deuce with him. There was something very awful, too, in the spectre's being provided with an infernal atmosphere of its own. Scrooge could not feel it himself, but this was clearly the case; for though the Ghost sat perfectly motionless, its hair, and skirts, and tassels, were still agitated as by the hot vapour from an oven.

"You see this toothpick?" said Scrooge, returning quickly to the charge, for the reason just assigned; and wishing, though it were only for a second, to divert the vision's stony gaze from himself.

"I do," replied the Ghost.

"You are not looking at it," said Scrooge.

"But I see it," said the Ghost, "notwithstanding."

"Well!" returned Scrooge, "I have but to swallow this, and be for the rest of my days persecuted by a legion of goblins, all of my own creation. Humbug, I tell you! humbug!"

At this the spirit raised a frightful cry, and shook its chain with such a dismal and appalling noise, that Scrooge held on tight to his chair, to save himself from falling in a swoon. But how much greater was his horror, when the phantom taking off the bandage round its head, as if it were too warm to wear indoors, its lower jaw dropped down upon its breast!

Scrooge fell upon his knees, and clasped his hands before his face.

"Mercy!" he said. "Dreadful apparition, why do you trouble me?"

"Man of the worldly mind!" replied the Ghost, "do you believe in me or not?"

"I do," said Scrooge. "I must. But why do spirits walk the earth, and why do they come to me?"

"It is required of every man," the Ghost returned, "that the spirit within him should walk abroad among his fellowmen, and travel far and wide; and if that spirit goes not forth in life, it is condemned to do so after death. It is doomed to wander through the world—oh, woe is me!—and witness what it cannot share, but might have shared on earth, and turned to happiness!"

Again the spectre raised a cry, and shook its chain and wrung its shadowy hands.

"You are fettered," said Scrooge, trembling. "Tell me why?"

"I wear the chain I forged in life," replied the Ghost. "I made it link by link, and yard by yard; I girded it on of my own free will, and of my own free will I wore it. Is its pattern strange to you?"

Scrooge trembled more and more.

"Or would you know," pursued the Ghost, "the weight and length of the strong coil you bear yourself? It was full as heavy and as long as this, seven Christmas Eves ago. You have laboured on it, since. It is a ponderous chain!"

Scrooge glanced about him on the floor, in the expectation of finding himself surrounded by some fifty or sixty fathoms of iron cable: but he could see nothing.

"Jacob," he said, imploringly. "Old Jacob Marley, tell me more. Speak comfort to me, Jacob!"

"I have none to give," the Ghost replied. "It comes from other regions, Ebenezer Scrooge, and is conveyed by other ministers, to other kinds of men. Nor can I tell you what I would. A very little more is all permitted to me. I cannot rest, I cannot stay, I cannot linger anywhere. My spirit never walked beyond our counting-house—mark me!—in life my spirit never roved beyond the narrow limits of our money-changing hole; and weary journeys lie before me!"

It was a habit with Scrooge, whenever he became thoughtful, to put his hands in his breeches pockets. Pondering on what the Ghost had said, he did so now, but without lifting up his eyes, or getting off his knees.

"You must have been very slow about it, Jacob," Scrooge observed, in a business-like manner, though with humility and deference.

"Slow!" the Ghost repeated.

"Seven years dead," mused Scrooge. "And travelling all the time!"

"The whole time," said the Ghost. "No rest, no peace. Incessant torture of remorse."

"You travel fast?" said Scrooge.

"On the wings of the wind," replied the Ghost.

"You might have got over a great quantity of ground in seven years," said Scrooge.

The Ghost, on hearing this, set up another cry, and clanked its chain so hideously in the dead silence of the night, that the Ward would have been justified in indicting it for a nuisance.

"Oh! captive, bound, and double-ironed," cried the phantom, "not to know, that ages of incessant labour by immortal creatures, for this earth must pass into eternity before the good of which it is susceptible is all developed. Not to know that any Christian spirit working kindly in its little sphere, whatever it may be, will find its mortal life too short for its vast means of usefulness. Not to know that no space of regret can make amends for one life's opportunity misused! Yet such was I! Oh! such was I!"

"But you were always a good man of business, Jacob," faltered Scrooge, who now began to apply this to himself.

"Business!" cried the Ghost, wringing its hands again. "Mankind was my business. The common welfare was my business; charity, mercy, forbearance, and benevolence, were, all, my business. The dealings of my trade were but a drop of water in the comprehensive ocean of my business!"

It held up its chain at arm's length, as if that were the cause of all its unavailing grief, and flung it heavily upon the ground again.

"At this time of the rolling year," the spectre said, "I suffer most. Why did I walk through crowds of fellow-beings with my eyes turned down, and never raise them to that blessed Star which led the Wise Men to a poor abode! Were there no poor homes to which its light would have conducted me!"

Scrooge was very much dismayed to hear the spectre going on at this rate, and began to quake exceedingly.

"Hear me!" cried the Ghost. "My time is nearly gone."

"I will," said Scrooge. "But don't be hard upon me! Don't be flowery, Jacob! Pray!"

"How it is that I appear before you in a shape that you can see, I may not tell. I have sat invisible beside you many and many a day."

It was not an agreeable idea. Scrooge shivered, and wiped the perspiration from his brow.

"That is no light part of my penance," pursued the Ghost. "I am here to-night to warn you, that you have yet a chance and hope of escaping my fate. A chance and hope of my procuring, Ebenezer."

"You were always a good friend to me," said Scrooge. "Thank'ee!"

"You will be haunted," resumed the Ghost, "by Three Spirits."

Scrooge's countenance fell almost as low as the Ghost's had done.

"Is that the chance and hope you mentioned, Jacob?" he demanded, in a faltering voice.

"It is."

"I—I think I'd rather not," said Scrooge.

"Without their visits," said the Ghost, "you cannot hope to shun the path I tread. Expect the first to-morrow, when the bell tolls One."

"Couldn't I take 'em all at once, and have it over, Jacob?" hinted Scrooge.

"Expect the second on the next night at the same hour. The third upon the next night when the last stroke of Twelve has ceased to vibrate. Look to see me no more; and look that, for your own sake, you remember what has passed between us!"

When it had said these words, the spectre took its wrapper from the table, and bound it round its head, as before. Scrooge knew this, by the smart sound its teeth made, when the jaws were brought together by the bandage. He ventured to raise his eyes again, and found his supernatural visitor confronting him in an erect attitude, with its chain wound over and about its arm.

The apparition walked backward from him; and at every step it took, the window raised itself a little, so that when the spectre reached it, it was wide open.

It beckoned Scrooge to approach, which he did. When they were within two paces of each other, Marley's Ghost held up its hand, warning him to come no nearer. Scrooge stopped.

Not so much in obedience, as in surprise and fear: for on the raising of the hand, he became sensible of confused noises in the air; incoherent sounds of lamentation and regret; wailings inexpressibly sorrowful and self-accusatory. The spectre, after listening for a moment, joined in the mournful dirge; and floated out upon the bleak, dark night.

Scrooge followed to the window: desperate in his curiosity. He looked out.

The air was filled with phantoms, wandering hither and thither in restless haste, and moaning as they went. Every one of them wore chains like Marley's Ghost; some few (they might be guilty governments) were linked together; none were free. Many had been personally known to Scrooge in their lives. He had been quite familiar with one old ghost, in a white waistcoat, with a monstrous iron safe attached to its ankle, who cried piteously at being unable to assist a wretched woman with an infant, whom it saw below, upon a door-step. The misery with them all was, clearly, that they sought to interfere, for good, in human matters, and had lost the power for ever.

Whether these creatures faded into mist, or mist enshrouded them, he could not tell. But they and their spirit voices faded together; and the night became as it had been when he walked home.

Scrooge closed the window, and examined the door by which the Ghost had entered. It was double-locked, as he had locked it with his own hands, and the bolts were undisturbed. He tried to say "Humbug!" but stopped at the first syllable. And being, from the emotion he had undergone, or the fatigues of the day, or his glimpse of the Invisible World, or the dull conversation of the Ghost, or the lateness of the hour, much in need of repose; went straight to bed, without undressing, and fell asleep upon the instant.

STAVE II: THE FIRST OF THE THREE SPIRITS

WHEN Scrooge awoke, it was so dark, that looking out of bed, he could scarcely distinguish the transparent window from the opaque walls of his chamber. He was endeavouring to pierce the darkness with his ferret eyes, when the chimes of a neighbouring church struck the four quarters. So he listened for the hour.

To his great astonishment the heavy bell went on from six to seven, and from seven to eight, and regularly up to twelve; then stopped. Twelve! It was past two when he went to bed. The clock was wrong. An icicle must have got into the works. Twelve!

He touched the spring of his repeater, to correct this most preposterous clock. Its rapid little pulse beat twelve: and stopped.

"Why, it isn't possible," said Scrooge, "that I can have slept through a whole day and far into another night. It isn't possible that anything has happened to the sun, and this is twelve at noon!"

The idea being an alarming one, he scrambled out of bed, and groped his way to the window. He was obliged to rub the frost off with the sleeve of his dressing-gown before he could see anything; and could see very little then. All he could make out was, that it was still very foggy and extremely cold, and that there was no noise of people running to and fro, and making a great stir, as there unquestionably would have been if night had beaten off bright day, and taken possession of the world. This was a great relief, because "three days after sight of this First of Exchange pay to Mr. Ebenezer Scrooge or his order," and so forth, would have become a mere United States' security if there were no days to count by.

Scrooge went to bed again, and thought, and thought, and thought it over and over and over, and could make nothing of it. The more he thought, the more perplexed he was; and the more he endeavoured not to think, the more he thought.

Marley's Ghost bothered him exceedingly. Every time he resolved within himself, after mature inquiry, that it was all a dream, his mind flew back again, like a strong spring released, to its first position, and presented the same problem to be worked all through, "Was it a dream or not?"

Scrooge lay in this state until the chime had gone three quarters more, when he remembered, on a sudden, that the Ghost had warned him of a visitation when the bell tolled one. He resolved to lie awake until the hour was passed; and, considering that he could no more go to sleep than go to Heaven, this was perhaps the wisest resolution in his power.

The quarter was so long, that he was more than once convinced he must have sunk into a doze unconsciously, and missed the clock. At length it broke upon his listening ear.

"Ding, dong!"

"A quarter past," said Scrooge, counting.

"Ding, dong!"

"Half-past!" said Scrooge.

"Ding, dong!"

"A quarter to it," said Scrooge.

"Ding, dong!"

"The hour itself," said Scrooge, triumphantly, "and nothing else!"

He spoke before the hour bell sounded, which it now did with a deep, dull, hollow, melancholy ONE. Light flashed up in the room upon the instant, and the curtains of his bed were drawn.

The curtains of his bed were drawn aside, I tell you, by a hand. Not the curtains at his feet, nor the curtains at his back, but those to which his face was addressed. The curtains of his bed were drawn aside; and Scrooge, starting up into a half-recumbent attitude, found himself face to face with the unearthly visitor who drew them: as close to it as I am now to you, and I am standing in the spirit at your elbow.

It was a strange figure—like a child: yet not so like a child as like an old man, viewed through some supernatural medium, which gave him the appearance of having receded from the view, and being diminished to a child's proportions. Its hair, which hung about its neck and down its back, was white as if with age; and yet the face had not a wrinkle in it, and the tenderest bloom was on the skin. The arms were very long and muscular; the hands the same, as if its hold were of uncommon strength. Its legs and feet, most delicately formed, were, like those upper members, bare. It wore a tunic of the purest white; and round its waist was bound a lustrous belt, the sheen of which was beautiful. It held a branch of fresh green holly in its hand; and, in singular contradiction of that wintry emblem, had its dress trimmed with summer flowers. But the strangest thing about it was, that from the crown of its head there sprung a bright clear jet of light, by which all this was visible; and which was doubtless the occasion of its using, in its duller moments, a great extinguisher for a cap, which it now held under its arm.

Even this, though, when Scrooge looked at it with increasing steadiness, was not its strangest quality. For as its belt sparkled and glittered now in one part and now in another, and what was light one instant, at another time was dark, so the figure itself fluctuated in its distinctness: being now a thing with one arm, now with one leg, now with twenty legs, now a pair of legs without a head, now a head without a body: of which dissolving parts, no outline would be visible in the dense gloom wherein they melted away. And in the very wonder of this, it would be itself again; distinct and clear as ever.

"Are you the Spirit, sir, whose coming was foretold to me?" asked Scrooge.

"I am!"

The voice was soft and gentle. Singularly low, as if instead of being so close beside him, it were at a distance.

"Who, and what are you?" Scrooge demanded.

"I am the Ghost of Christmas Past."

"Long Past?" inquired Scrooge: observant of its dwarfish stature.

"No. Your past."

Perhaps, Scrooge could not have told anybody why, if anybody could have asked him; but he had a special desire to see the Spirit in his cap; and begged him to be covered.

"What!" exclaimed the Ghost, "would you so soon put out, with worldly hands, the light I give? Is it not enough that you are one of those whose passions made this cap, and force me through whole trains of years to wear it low upon my brow!"

Scrooge reverently disclaimed all intention to offend or any knowledge of having wilfully "bonneted" the Spirit at any period of his life. He then made bold to inquire what business brought him there.

"Your welfare!" said the Ghost.

Scrooge expressed himself much obliged, but could not help thinking that a night of unbroken rest would have been more conducive to that end. The Spirit must have heard him thinking, for it said immediately:

"Your reclamation, then. Take heed!"

It put out its strong hand as it spoke, and clasped him gently by the arm.

"Rise! and walk with me!"

It would have been in vain for Scrooge to plead that the weather and the hour were not adapted to pedestrian purposes; that bed was warm, and the thermometer a long way below freezing; that he was clad but lightly in his slippers, dressing-gown, and nightcap; and that he had a cold upon him at that time. The grasp, though gentle as a woman's hand, was not to be resisted. He rose: but finding that the Spirit made towards the window, clasped his robe in supplication.

"I am a mortal," Scrooge remonstrated, "and liable to fall."

"Bear but a touch of my hand there," said the Spirit, laying it upon his heart, "and you shall be upheld in more than this!"

As the words were spoken, they passed through the wall, and stood upon an open country road, with fields on either hand. The city had entirely vanished. Not a vestige of it was to be seen. The darkness and the mist had vanished with it, for it was a clear, cold, winter day, with snow upon the ground.

"Good Heaven!" said Scrooge, clasping his hands together, as he looked about him. "I was bred in this place. I was a boy here!"

The Spirit gazed upon him mildly. Its gentle touch, though it had been light and instantaneous, appeared still present to the old man's sense of feeling. He was conscious of a thousand odours floating in the air, each one connected with a thousand thoughts, and hopes, and joys, and cares long, long, forgotten!

"Your lip is trembling," said the Ghost. "And what is that upon your cheek?"

Scrooge muttered, with an unusual catching in his voice, that it was a pimple; and begged the Ghost to lead him where he would.

"You recollect the way?" inquired the Spirit.

"Remember it!" cried Scrooge with fervour; "I could walk it blindfold."

"Strange to have forgotten it for so many years!" observed the Ghost. "Let us go on."

They walked along the road, Scrooge recognising every gate, and post, and tree; until a little market-town appeared in the distance, with its bridge, its church, and winding river. Some shaggy ponies now were seen trotting towards them with boys upon their backs, who called to other boys in country gigs and carts, driven by farmers. All these boys were in great spirits, and shouted to each other, until the broad fields were so full of merry music, that the crisp air laughed to hear it!

"These are but shadows of the things that have been," said the Ghost. "They have no consciousness of us."

The jocund travellers came on; and as they came, Scrooge knew and named them every one. Why was he rejoiced beyond all bounds to see them! Why did his cold eye glisten, and his heart leap up as they went past! Why was he filled with gladness when he heard them give each other Merry Christmas, as they parted at cross-roads and bye-ways, for their several homes! What was merry Christmas to Scrooge? Out upon merry Christmas! What good had it ever done to him?

"The school is not quite deserted," said the Ghost. "A solitary child, neglected by his friends, is left there still."

Scrooge said he knew it. And he sobbed.

They left the high-road, by a well-remembered lane, and soon approached a mansion of dull red brick, with a little weathercock-surmounted cupola, on the roof, and a bell hanging in it. It was a large house, but one of broken fortunes; for the spacious offices were little used, their walls were damp and mossy, their windows broken, and their gates decayed. Fowls clucked and strutted in the stables; and the coach-houses and sheds were over-run with grass. Nor was it more retentive of its ancient state, within; for entering the dreary hall, and glancing through the open doors of many rooms, they found them poorly furnished, cold, and vast. There was an earthy savour in the air, a chilly bareness in the place, which associated itself somehow with too much getting up by candle-light, and not too much to eat.

They went, the Ghost and Scrooge, across the hall, to a door at the back of the house. It opened before them, and disclosed a long, bare, melancholy room, made barer still by lines of plain deal forms and desks. At one of these a lonely boy was reading near a feeble fire; and Scrooge sat down upon a form, and wept to see his poor forgotten self as he used to be.

Not a latent echo in the house, not a squeak and scuffle from the mice behind the panelling, not a drip from the half-thawed water-spout in the dull yard behind, not a sigh among the leafless boughs of one despondent poplar, not the idle swinging of an empty store-house door, no, not a clicking in the fire, but fell upon the heart of Scrooge with a softening influence, and gave a freer passage to his tears.

The Spirit touched him on the arm, and pointed to his younger self, intent upon his reading. Suddenly a man, in foreign garments: wonderfully real and distinct to look at: stood outside the window, with an axe stuck in his belt, and leading by the bridle an ass laden with wood.

"Why, it's Ali Baba!" Scrooge exclaimed in ecstasy. "It's dear old honest Ali Baba! Yes, yes, I know! One Christmas time, when yonder solitary child was left here all alone, he did come, for the first time, just like that. Poor boy! And Valentine," said Scrooge, "and his wild brother, Orson; there they go!

And what's his name, who was put down in his drawers, asleep, at the Gate of Damascus; don't you see him! And the Sultan's Groom turned upside down by the Genii; there he is upon his head! Serve him right. I'm glad of it. What business had he to be married to the Princess!"

To hear Scrooge expending all the earnestness of his nature on such subjects, in a most extraordinary voice between laughing and crying; and to see his heightened and excited face; would have been a surprise to his business friends in the city, indeed.

"There's the Parrot!" cried Scrooge. "Green body and yellow tail, with a thing like a lettuce growing out of the top of his head; there he is! Poor Robin Crusoe, he called him, when he came home again after sailing round the island. 'Poor Robin Crusoe, where have you been, Robin Crusoe?' The man thought he was dreaming, but he wasn't. It was the Parrot, you know. There goes Friday, running for his life to the little creek! Halloa! Hoop! Halloo!"

Then, with a rapidity of transition very foreign to his usual character, he said, in pity for his former self, "Poor boy!" and cried again.

"I wish," Scrooge muttered, putting his hand in his pocket, and looking about him, after drying his eyes with his cuff: "but it's too late now."

"What is the matter?" asked the Spirit.

"Nothing," said Scrooge. "Nothing. There was a boy singing a Christmas Carol at my door last night. I should like to have given him something: that's all."

The Ghost smiled thoughtfully, and waved its hand: saying as it did so, "Let us see another Christmas!"

Scrooge's former self grew larger at the words, and the room became a little darker and more dirty. The panels shrunk, the windows cracked; fragments of plaster fell out of the ceiling, and the naked laths were shown instead; but how all this was brought about, Scrooge knew no more than you do. He only knew that it was quite correct; that everything had happened so; that there he was, alone again, when all the other boys had gone home for the jolly holidays.

He was not reading now, but walking up and down despairingly. Scrooge looked at the Ghost, and with a mournful shaking of his head, glanced anxiously towards the door.

It opened; and a little girl, much younger than the boy, came darting in, and putting her arms about his neck, and often kissing him, addressed him as her "Dear, dear brother."

"I have come to bring you home, dear brother!" said the child, clapping her tiny hands, and bending down to laugh. "To bring you home, home, home!"

"Home, little Fan?" returned the boy.

"Yes!" said the child, brimful of glee. "Home, for good and all. Home, for ever and ever. Father is so much kinder than he used to be, that home's like Heaven! He spoke so gently to me one dear night when I was going to bed, that I was not afraid to ask him once more if you might come home; and he said Yes, you should; and sent me in a coach to bring you. And you're to be a man!" said the child, opening her eyes, "and are never to come back here; but first, we're to be together all the Christmas long, and have the merriest time in all the world."

"You are quite a woman, little Fan!" exclaimed the boy.

She clapped her hands and laughed, and tried to touch his

head; but being too little, laughed again, and stood on tiptoe to embrace him. Then she began to drag him, in her childish eagerness, towards the door; and he, nothing loth to go, accompanied her.

A terrible voice in the hall cried, "Bring down Master Scrooge's box, there!" and in the hall appeared the schoolmaster himself, who glared on Master Scrooge with a ferocious condescension, and threw him into a dreadful state of mind by shaking hands with him. He then conveyed him and his sister into the veriest old well of a shivering best-parlour that ever was seen, where the maps upon the wall, and the celestial and terrestrial globes in the windows, were waxy with cold. Here he produced a decanter of curiously light wine, and a block of curiously heavy cake, and administered instalments of those dainties to the young people: at the same time, sending out a meagre servant to offer a glass of "something" to the postboy, who answered that he thanked the gentleman, but if it was the same tap as he had tasted before, he had rather not. Master Scrooge's trunk being by this time tied on to the top of the chaise, the children bade the schoolmaster good-bye right willingly; and getting into it, drove gaily down the garden-sweep: the quick wheels dashing the hoar-frost and snow from off the dark leaves of the evergreens like spray.

"Always a delicate creature, whom a breath might have withered," said the Ghost. "But she had a large heart!"

"So she had," cried Scrooge. "You're right. I will not gainsay it, Spirit. God forbid!"

"She died a woman," said the Ghost, "and had, as I think, children."

"One child," Scrooge returned.

"True," said the Ghost. "Your nephew!"

Scrooge seemed uneasy in his mind; and answered briefly, "Yes."

Although they had but that moment left the school behind them, they were now in the busy thoroughfares of a city, where shadowy passengers passed and repassed; where shadowy carts and coaches battled for the way, and all the strife and tumult of a real city were. It was made plain enough, by the dressing of the shops, that here too it was Christmas time again; but it was evening, and the streets were lighted up.

The Ghost stopped at a certain warehouse door, and asked Scrooge if he knew it.

"Know it!" said Scrooge. "Was I apprenticed here!"

They went in. At sight of an old gentleman in a Welsh wig, sitting behind such a high desk, that if he had been two inches taller he must have knocked his head against the ceiling, Scrooge cried in great excitement:

"Why, it's old Fezziwig! Bless his heart; it's Fezziwig alive again!"

Old Fezziwig laid down his pen, and looked up at the clock, which pointed to the hour of seven. He rubbed his hands; adjusted his capacious waistcoat; laughed all over himself, from his shoes to his organ of benevolence; and called out in a comfortable, oily, rich, fat, jovial voice:

"Yo ho, there! Ebenezer! Dick!"

Scrooge's former self, now grown a young man, came briskly in, accompanied by his fellow-'prentice.

"Dick Wilkins, to be sure!" said Scrooge to the Ghost.

"Bless me, yes. There he is. He was very much attached to me, was Dick. Poor Dick! Dear, dear!"

"Yo ho, my boys!" said Fezziwig. "No more work to-night. Christmas Eve, Dick. Christmas, Ebenezer! Let's have the shutters up," cried old Fezziwig, with a sharp clap of his hands, "before a man can say Jack Robinson!"

You wouldn't believe how those two fellows went at it! They charged into the street with the shutters–one, two, three–had 'em up in their places–four, five, six–barred 'em and pinned 'em–seven, eight, nine–and came back before you could have got to twelve, panting like race-horses.

"Hilli-ho!" cried old Fezziwig, skipping down from the high desk, with wonderful agility. "Clear away, my lads, and let's have lots of room here! Hilli-ho, Dick! Chirrup, Ebenezer!"

Clear away! There was nothing they wouldn't have cleared away, or couldn't have cleared away, with old Fezziwig looking on. It was done in a minute. Every movable was packed off, as if it were dismissed from public life for evermore; the floor was swept and watered, the lamps were trimmed, fuel was heaped upon the fire; and the warehouse was as snug, and warm, and dry, and bright a ball-room, as you would desire to see upon a winter's night.

In came a fiddler with a music-book, and went up to the lofty desk, and made an orchestra of it, and tuned like fifty stomach-aches. In came Mrs. Fezziwig, one vast substantial smile. In came the three Miss Fezziwigs, beaming and lovable. In came the six young followers whose hearts they broke. In came all the young men and women employed in the business.

In came the housemaid, with her cousin, the baker. In came the cook, with her brother's particular friend, the milkman. In came the boy from over the way, who was suspected of not having board enough from his master; trying to hide himself behind the girl from next door but one, who was proved to have had her ears pulled by her mistress. In they all came, one after another; some shyly, some boldly, some gracefully, some awkwardly, some pushing, some pulling; in they all came, anyhow and everyhow. Away they all went, twenty couple at once; hands half round and back again the other way; down the middle and up again; round and round in various stages of affectionate grouping; old top couple always turning up in the wrong place; new top couple starting off again, as soon as they got there; all top couples at last, and not a bottom one to help them! When this result was brought about, old Fez-ziwig, clapping his hands to stop the dance, cried out, "Well done!" and the fiddler plunged his hot face into a pot of porter, especially provided for that purpose. But scorning rest, upon his reappearance, he instantly began again, though there were no dancers yet, as if the other fiddler had been carried home, exhausted, on a shutter, and he were a bran-new man resolved to beat him out of sight, or perish.

There were more dances, and there were forfeits, and more dances, and there was cake, and there was negus, and there was a great piece of Cold Roast, and there was a great piece of Cold Boiled, and there were mince-pies, and plenty of beer. But the great effect of the evening came after the Roast and Boiled, when the fiddler (an artful dog, mind! The sort of man who knew his business better than you or I could have told it him!)

struck up "Sir Roger de Coverley." Then old Fezziwig stood out
to dance with Mrs. Fezziwig. Top couple, too; with a good stiff
piece of work cut out for them; three or four and twenty pair
of partners; people who were not to be trifled with; people who
would dance, and had no notion of walking.

But if they had been twice as many—ah, four times—old
Fezziwig would have been a match for them, and so would
Mrs. Fezziwig. As to her, she was worthy to be his partner in
every sense of the term. If that's not high praise, tell me higher,
and I'll use it. A positive light appeared to issue from Fezziwig's
calves. They shone in every part of the dance like moons. You
couldn't have predicted, at any given time, what would have
become of them next. And when old Fezziwig and Mrs. Fezziwig had gone all through the dance; advance and retire, both
hands to your partner, bow and curtsey, corkscrew, thread-the-
needle, and back again to your place; Fezziwig "cut"—cut so
deftly, that he appeared to wink with his legs, and came upon
his feet again without a stagger.

When the clock struck eleven, this domestic ball broke up.
Mr. and Mrs. Fezziwig took their stations, one on either side
of the door, and shaking hands with every person individually
as he or she went out, wished him or her a Merry Christmas.
When everybody had retired but the two 'prentices, they did
the same to them; and thus the cheerful voices died away, and
the lads were left to their beds; which were under a counter in
the back-shop.

During the whole of this time, Scrooge had acted like a
man out of his wits. His heart and soul were in the scene, and
with his former self. He corroborated everything, remembered

everything, enjoyed everything, and underwent the strangest agitation. It was not until now, when the bright faces of his former self and Dick were turned from them, that he remembered the Ghost, and became conscious that it was looking full upon him, while the light upon its head burnt very clear.

"A small matter," said the Ghost, "to make these silly folks so full of gratitude."

"Small!" echoed Scrooge.

The Spirit signed to him to listen to the two apprentices, who were pouring out their hearts in praise of Fezziwig: and when he had done so, said,

"Why! Is it not? He has spent but a few pounds of your mortal money: three or four perhaps. Is that so much that he deserves this praise?"

"It isn't that," said Scrooge, heated by the remark, and speaking unconsciously like his former, not his latter, self. "It isn't that, Spirit. He has the power to render us happy or unhappy; to make our service light or burdensome; a pleasure or a toil. Say that his power lies in words and looks; in things so slight and insignificant that it is impossible to add and count 'em up: what then? The happiness he gives, is quite as great as if it cost a fortune."

He felt the Spirit's glance, and stopped.

"What is the matter?" asked the Ghost.

"Nothing particular," said Scrooge.

"Something, I think?" the Ghost insisted.

"No," said Scrooge, "No. I should like to be able to say a word or two to my clerk just now. That's all."

His former self turned down the lamps as he gave utterance

to the wish; and Scrooge and the Ghost again stood side by side in the open air.

"My time grows short," observed the Spirit. "Quick!"

This was not addressed to Scrooge, or to any one whom he could see, but it produced an immediate effect. For again Scrooge saw himself. He was older now; a man in the prime of life. His face had not the harsh and rigid lines of later years; but it had begun to wear the signs of care and avarice. There was an eager, greedy, restless motion in the eye, which showed the passion that had taken root, and where the shadow of the growing tree would fall.

He was not alone, but sat by the side of a fair young girl in a mourning-dress: in whose eyes there were tears, which sparkled in the light that shone out of the Ghost of Christmas Past.

"It matters little," she said, softly. "To you, very little. Another idol has displaced me; and if it can cheer and comfort you in time to come, as I would have tried to do, I have no just cause to grieve."

"What Idol has displaced you?" he rejoined.

"A golden one."

"This is the even-handed dealing of the world!" he said. "There is nothing on which it is so hard as poverty; and there is nothing it professes to condemn with such severity as the pursuit of wealth!"

"You fear the world too much," she answered, gently. "All your other hopes have merged into the hope of being beyond the chance of its sordid reproach. I have seen your nobler aspirations fall off one by one, until the master-passion, Gain, engrosses you. Have I not?"

"What then?" he retorted. "Even if I have grown so much wiser, what then? I am not changed towards you."

She shook her head.

"Am I?"

"Our contract is an old one. It was made when we were both poor and content to be so, until, in good season, we could improve our worldly fortune by our patient industry. You are changed. When it was made, you were another man."

"I was a boy," he said impatiently.

"Your own feeling tells you that you were not what you are," she returned. "I am. That which promised happiness when we were one in heart, is fraught with misery now that we are two. How often and how keenly I have thought of this, I will not say. It is enough that I have thought of it, and can release you."

"Have I ever sought release?"

"In words. No. Never."

"In what, then?"

"In a changed nature; in an altered spirit; in another atmosphere of life; another Hope as its great end. In everything that made my love of any worth or value in your sight. If this had never been between us," said the girl, looking mildly, but with steadiness, upon him; "tell me, would you seek me out and try to win me now? Ah, no!"

He seemed to yield to the justice of this supposition, in spite of himself. But he said with a struggle, "You think not."

"I would gladly think otherwise if I could," she answered, "Heaven knows! When I have learned a Truth like this, I know how strong and irresistible it must be. But if you were free to-day, to-morrow, yesterday, can even I believe that you would choose a dowerless girl—you who, in your very confidence with her, weigh everything by Gain: or, choosing her, if for a moment you were false enough to your one guiding principle to do so, do I not know that your repentance and regret would surely follow? I do; and I release you. With a full heart, for the love of him you once were."

He was about to speak; but with her head turned from him, she resumed.

"You may—the memory of what is past half makes me hope you will—have pain in this. A very, very brief time, and you will dismiss the recollection of it, gladly, as an unprofitable dream, from which it happened well that you awoke. May you be happy in the life you have chosen!"

She left him, and they parted.

"Spirit!" said Scrooge, "show me no more! Conduct me home. Why do you delight to torture me?"

"One shadow more!" exclaimed the Ghost.

"No more!" cried Scrooge. "No more. I don't wish to see it. Show me no more!"

But the relentless Ghost pinioned him in both his arms, and forced him to observe what happened next.

They were in another scene and place; a room, not very large or handsome, but full of comfort. Near to the winter fire sat a beautiful young girl, so like that last that Scrooge believed it was the same, until he saw her, now a comely matron, sitting opposite her daughter. The noise in this room was perfectly tumultuous, for there were more children there, than Scrooge in his agitated state of mind could count; and, unlike the celebrated herd in the poem, they were not forty children conducting themselves like one, but every child was conducting itself like forty. The consequences were uproarious beyond belief; but no one seemed to care; on the contrary, the mother and daughter laughed heartily, and enjoyed it very much; and the latter, soon beginning to mingle in the sports, got pillaged by the young brigands most ruthlessly. What would I not have given to be one of them! Though I never could have been so rude, no, no! I wouldn't for the wealth of all the world have crushed that braided hair, and torn it down; and for the precious little shoe, I wouldn't have plucked it off, God bless my soul! to save my life. As to measuring her waist in sport, as they did, bold young brood, I couldn't have done it; I should have expected my arm to have grown round it for a punishment, and never come straight again. And yet I should have dearly liked, I own, to have touched her lips; to have questioned her, that she might have opened them; to have looked upon the lashes of her downcast eyes, and never raised a blush; to have let loose waves of hair, an inch of which would be a keepsake beyond price: in short, I should have liked, I do confess, to have had the lightest licence of a child, and yet to have been man enough to know its value.

But now a knocking at the door was heard, and such a rush immediately ensued that she with laughing face and plundered dress was borne towards it the centre of a flushed and boisterous group, just in time to greet the father, who came home attended by a man laden with Christmas toys and presents. Then the shouting and the struggling, and the onslaught that was made on the defenceless porter! The scaling him with chairs for ladders to dive into his pockets, despoil him of brown-paper parcels, hold on tight by his cravat, hug him round his neck, pommel his back, and kick his legs in irrepressible affection! The shouts of wonder and delight with which the development of every package was received! The terrible announcement that the baby had been taken in the act of putting a doll's frying-pan into his mouth, and was more than suspected of having swallowed a fictitious turkey, glued on a wooden platter! The immense relief of finding this a false alarm! The joy, and gratitude, and ecstasy! They are all indescribable alike. It is enough that by degrees the children and their emotions got out of the parlour, and by one stair at a time, up to the top of the house; where they went to bed, and so subsided.

And now Scrooge looked on more attentively than ever, when the master of the house, having his daughter leaning fondly on him, sat down with her and her mother at his own fireside; and when he thought that such another creature, quite as graceful and as full of promise, might have called him father, and been a spring-time in the haggard winter of his life, his sight grew very dim indeed.

"Belle," said the husband, turning to his wife with a smile, "I saw an old friend of yours this afternoon."

"Who was it?"

"Guess!"

"How can I? Tut, don't I know?" she added in the same breath, laughing as he laughed. "Mr. Scrooge."

"Mr. Scrooge it was. I passed his office window; and as it was not shut up, and he had a candle inside, I could scarcely help seeing him. His partner lies upon the point of death, I hear; and there he sat alone. Quite alone in the world, I do believe."

"Spirit!" said Scrooge in a broken voice, "remove me from this place."

"I told you these were shadows of the things that have been," said the Ghost. "That they are what they are, do not blame me!"

"Remove me!" Scrooge exclaimed, "I cannot bear it!"

He turned upon the Ghost, and seeing that it looked upon him with a face, in which in some strange way there were fragments of all the faces it had shown him, wrestled with it.

"Leave me! Take me back. Haunt me no longer!"

In the struggle, if that can be called a struggle in which the Ghost with no visible resistance on its own part was undisturbed by any effort of its adversary, Scrooge observed that its light was burning high and bright; and dimly connecting that with its influence over him, he seized the extinguisher-cap, and by a sudden action pressed it down upon its head.

The Spirit dropped beneath it, so that the extinguisher covered its whole form; but though Scrooge pressed it down with all his force, he could not hide the light: which streamed from under it, in an unbroken flood upon the ground.

He was conscious of being exhausted, and overcome by an irresistible drowsiness; and, further, of being in his own bedroom. He gave the cap a parting squeeze, in which his hand relaxed; and had barely time to reel to bed, before he sank into a heavy sleep.

STAVE III: THE SECOND OF
THE THREE SPIRITS

AWAKING in the middle of a prodigiously tough snore, and sitting up in bed to get his thoughts together, Scrooge had no occasion to be told that the bell was again upon the stroke of One. He felt that he was restored to consciousness in the right nick of time, for the especial purpose of holding a conference with the second messenger despatched to him through Jacob Marley's intervention. But finding that he turned uncomfortably cold when he began to wonder which of his curtains this new spectre would draw back, he put them every one aside with his own hands; and lying down again, established a sharp look-out all round the bed. For he wished to challenge the Spirit on the moment of its appearance, and did not wish to be taken by surprise, and made nervous.

Gentlemen of the free-and-easy sort, who plume themselves on being acquainted with a move or two, and being usually equal to the time-of-day, express the wide range of their capacity for adventure by observing that they are good for anything from pitch-and-toss to manslaughter; between which opposite extremes, no doubt, there lies a tolerably wide and comprehensive range of subjects. Without venturing for Scrooge quite as hardily as this, I don't mind calling on you to believe that he was ready for a good broad field of strange appearances, and that nothing between a baby and rhinoceros would have astonished him very much.

Now, being prepared for almost anything, he was not by any means prepared for nothing; and, consequently, when the Bell struck One, and no shape appeared, he was taken with a violent fit of trembling. Five minutes, ten minutes, a quarter of an hour went by, yet nothing came. All this time, he lay upon his bed, the very core and centre of a blaze of ruddy light, which streamed upon it when the clock proclaimed the hour; and which, being only light, was more alarming than a dozen ghosts, as he was powerless to make out what it meant, or would be at; and was sometimes apprehensive that he might be at that very moment an interesting case of spontaneous combustion, without having the consolation of knowing it. At last, however, he began to think—as you or I would have thought at first; for it is always the person not in the predicament who knows what ought to have been done in it, and would unquestionably have done it too—at last, I say, he began to think that the source and secret of this ghostly light might be in the adjoining room, from whence, on further tracing it, it seemed to shine. This idea taking full possession of his mind, he got up softly and shuffled in his slippers to the door.

The moment Scrooge's hand was on the lock, a strange voice called him by his name, and bade him enter. He obeyed.

It was his own room. There was no doubt about that. But it had undergone a surprising transformation. The walls and ceiling were so hung with living green, that it looked a perfect grove; from every part of which, bright gleaming berries glistened. The crisp leaves of holly, mistletoe, and ivy reflected back the light, as if so many little mirrors had been scattered there; and such a mighty blaze went roaring up the chimney, as that dull petrification of a hearth had never known in Scrooge's time, or Marley's, or for many and many a winter season gone. Heaped up on the floor, to form a kind of throne, were turkeys, geese, game, poultry, brawn, great joints of meat, sucking-pigs, long wreaths of sausages, mince-pies, plum-puddings, barrels of oysters, red-hot chestnuts, cherry-cheeked apples, juicy oranges, luscious pears, immense twelfth-cakes, and seething bowls of punch, that made the chamber dim with their delicious steam. In easy state upon this couch, there sat a jolly Giant, glorious to see; who bore a glowing torch, in shape not unlike Plenty's horn, and held it up, high up, to shed its light on Scrooge, as he came peeping round the door.

"Come in!" exclaimed the Ghost. "Come in! and know me better, man!"

Scrooge entered timidly, and hung his head before this Spirit. He was not the dogged Scrooge he had been; and though the Spirit's eyes were clear and kind, he did not like to meet them.

"I am the Ghost of Christmas Present," said the Spirit. "Look upon me!"

Scrooge reverently did so. It was clothed in one simple green robe, or mantle, bordered with white fur. This garment hung so loosely on the figure, that its capacious breast was bare, as if disdaining to be warded or concealed by any artifice. Its feet, observable beneath the ample folds of the garment, were also bare; and on its head it wore no other covering than a holly wreath, set here and there with shining icicles. Its dark brown curls were long and free; free as its genial face, its sparkling eye, its open hand, its cheery voice, its unconstrained demeanour, and its joyful air. Girded round its middle was an antique scabbard; but no sword was in it, and the ancient sheath was eaten up with rust.

"You have never seen the like of me before!" exclaimed the Spirit.

"Never," Scrooge made answer to it.

"Have never walked forth with the younger members of my family; meaning (for I am very young) my elder brothers born in these later years?" pursued the Phantom.

"I don't think I have," said Scrooge. "I am afraid I have not. Have you had many brothers, Spirit?"

"More than eighteen hundred," said the Ghost.

"A tremendous family to provide for!" muttered Scrooge.

The Ghost of Christmas Present rose.

"Spirit," said Scrooge submissively, "conduct me where you will. I went forth last night on compulsion, and I learnt a lesson which is working now. To-night, if you have aught to teach me, let me profit by it."

"Touch my robe!"

Scrooge did as he was told, and held it fast.

Holly, mistletoe, red berries, ivy, turkeys, geese, game, poultry, brawn, meat, pigs, sausages, oysters, pies, puddings, fruit, and punch, all vanished instantly. So did the room, the fire, the ruddy glow, the hour of night, and they stood in the city streets on Christmas morning, where (for the weather was severe) the people made a rough, but brisk and not unpleasant kind of music, in scraping the snow from the pavement in front of their dwellings, and from the tops of their houses, whence it was mad delight to the boys to see it come plumping down into the road below, and splitting into artificial little snow-storms.

The house fronts looked black enough, and the windows blacker, contrasting with the smooth white sheet of snow upon the roofs, and with the dirtier snow upon the ground; which last deposit had been ploughed up in deep furrows by the heavy wheels of carts and waggons; furrows that crossed and re-crossed each other hundreds of times where the great streets branched off; and made intricate channels, hard to trace in the thick yellow mud and icy water. The sky was gloomy, and the shortest streets were choked up with a dingy mist, half thawed, half frozen, whose heavier particles descended in a shower of sooty atoms, as if all the chimneys in Great Britain had, by one consent, caught fire, and were blazing away to their dear hearts' content. There was nothing very cheerful in the climate or the town, and yet was there an air of cheerfulness abroad that the clearest summer air and brightest summer sun might have endeavoured to diffuse in vain.

For, the people who were shovelling away on the housetops were jovial and full of glee; calling out to one another from the

parapets, and now and then exchanging a facetious snowball—
better-natured missile far than many a wordy jest— laughing
heartily if it went right and not less heartily if it went wrong.
The poulterers' shops were still half open, and the fruiterers'
were radiant in their glory. There were great, round, pot-bel-
lied baskets of chestnuts, shaped like the waistcoats of jolly
old gentlemen, lolling at the doors, and tumbling out into the
street in their apoplectic opulence. There were ruddy, brown-
faced, broad-girthed Spanish Onions, shining in the fatness
of their growth like Spanish Friars, and winking from their
shelves in wanton slyness at the girls as they went by, and
glanced demurely at the hung-up mistletoe. There were pears
and apples, clustered high in blooming pyramids; there were
bunches of grapes, made, in the shopkeepers' benevolence to
dangle from conspicuous hooks, that people's mouths might
water gratis as they passed; there were piles of filberts, mossy
and brown, recalling, in their fragrance, ancient walks among
the woods, and pleasant shufflings ankle deep through withered leaves; there were Norfolk Biffins, squat and swarthy, setting off the yellow of the oranges and lemons, and, in the great
compactness of their juicy persons, urgently entreating and
beseeching to be carried home in paper bags and eaten after
dinner. The very gold and silver fish, set forth among these
choice fruits in a bowl, though members of a dull and stag-
nant-blooded race, appeared to know that there was something
going on; and, to a fish, went gasping round and round their
little world in slow and passionless excitement.

The Grocers'! oh, the Grocers'! nearly closed, with perhaps two shutters down, or one; but through those gaps such

glimpses! It was not alone that the scales descending on the counter made a merry sound, or that the twine and roller parted company so briskly, or that the canisters were rattled up and down like juggling tricks, or even that the blended scents of tea and coffee were so grateful to the nose, or even that the raisins were so plentiful and rare, the almonds so extremely white, the sticks of cinnamon so long and straight, the other spices so delicious, the candied fruits so caked and spotted with molten sugar as to make the coldest lookers-on feel faint and subsequently bilious. Nor was it that the figs were moist and pulpy, or that the French plums blushed in modest tartness from their highly-decorated boxes, or that everything was good to eat and in its Christmas dress; but the customers were all so hurried and so eager in the hopeful promise of the day, that they tumbled up against each other at the door, crashing their wicker baskets wildly, and left their purchases upon the counter, and came running back to fetch them, and committed hundreds of the like mistakes, in the best humour possible; while the Grocer and his people were so frank and fresh that the polished hearts with which they fastened their aprons behind might have been their own, worn outside for general inspection, and for Christmas daws to peck at if they chose.

But soon the steeples called good people all, to church and chapel, and away they came, flocking through the streets in their best clothes, and with their gayest faces. And at the same time there emerged from scores of bye-streets, lanes, and nameless turnings, innumerable people, carrying their dinners to the bakers' shops. The sight of these poor revellers appeared to interest the Spirit very much, for he stood with Scrooge beside him in a baker's doorway, and taking off the covers as their bearers passed, sprinkled incense on their dinners from his torch. And it was a very uncommon kind of torch, for once or twice when there were angry words between some dinner-carriers who had jostled each other, he shed a few drops of water on them from it, and their good humour was restored directly. For they said, it was a shame to quarrel upon Christmas Day. And so it was! God love it, so it was!

In time the bells ceased, and the bakers were shut up; and yet there was a genial shadowing forth of all these dinners and the progress of their cooking, in the thawed blotch of wet above each baker's oven; where the pavement smoked as if its stones were cooking too.

"Is there a peculiar flavour in what you sprinkle from your torch?" asked Scrooge.

"There is. My own."

"Would it apply to any kind of dinner on this day?" asked Scrooge.

"To any kindly given. To a poor one most."

"Why to a poor one most?" asked Scrooge.

"Because it needs it most."

"Spirit," said Scrooge, after a moment's thought, "I wonder you, of all the beings in the many worlds about us, should desire to cramp these people's opportunities of innocent enjoyment."

"I!" cried the Spirit.

"You would deprive them of their means of dining every seventh day, often the only day on which they can be said to dine at all," said Scrooge. "Wouldn't you?"

"I!" cried the Spirit.

"You seek to close these places on the Seventh Day?" said Scrooge. "And it comes to the same thing."

"I seek!" exclaimed the Spirit.

"Forgive me if I am wrong. It has been done in your name, or at least in that of your family," said Scrooge.

"There are some upon this earth of yours," returned the Spirit, "who lay claim to know us, and who do their deeds of passion, pride, ill-will, hatred, envy, bigotry, and selfishness in our name, who are as strange to us and all our kith and kin, as if they had never lived. Remember that, and charge their doings on themselves, not us."

Scrooge promised that he would; and they went on, invisible, as they had been before, into the suburbs of the town. It was a remarkable quality of the Ghost (which Scrooge had observed at the baker's), that notwithstanding his gigantic size, he could accommodate himself to any place with ease; and that he stood beneath a low roof quite as gracefully and like a supernatural creature, as it was possible he could have done in any lofty hall.

And perhaps it was the pleasure the good Spirit had in showing off this power of his, or else it was his own kind, generous, hearty nature, and his sympathy with all poor men, that led him straight to Scrooge's clerk's; for there he went, and took Scrooge with him, holding to his robe; and on the threshold of the door the Spirit smiled, and stopped to bless Bob Cratchit's dwelling with the sprinkling of his torch. Think of that! Bob had but fifteen "Bob" a-week himself; he pocketed on Saturdays but fifteen copies of his Christian name; and yet the Ghost of Christmas Present blessed his four-roomed house!

Then up rose Mrs. Cratchit, Cratchit's wife, dressed out but poorly in a twice-turned gown, but brave in ribbons, which are cheap and make a goodly show for sixpence; and she laid the cloth, assisted by Belinda Cratchit, second of her daughters, also brave in ribbons; while Master Peter Cratchit plunged a fork into the saucepan of potatoes, and getting the corners of his monstrous shirt collar (Bob's private property, conferred upon his son and heir in honour of the day) into his mouth, rejoiced to find himself so gallantly attired, and yearned to show his linen in the fashionable Parks. And now two smaller Cratchits, boy and girl, came tearing in, screaming that outside the baker's they had smelt the goose, and known it for their own; and basking in luxurious thoughts of sage and onion, these young Cratchits danced about the table, and exalted Master Peter Cratchit to the skies, while he (not proud, although his collars nearly choked him) blew the fire, until the slow potatoes bubbling up, knocked loudly at the saucepan-lid to be let out and peeled.

"What has ever got your precious father then?" said Mrs. Cratchit. "And your brother, Tiny Tim! And Martha warn't as late last Christmas Day by half-an-hour?"

"Here's Martha, mother!" said a girl, appearing as she spoke.

"Here's Martha, mother!" cried the two young Cratchits. "Hurrah! There's such a goose, Martha!"

"Why, bless your heart alive, my dear, how late you are!" said Mrs. Cratchit, kissing her a dozen times, and taking off her shawl and bonnet for her with officious zeal.

"We'd a deal of work to finish up last night," replied the

girl, "and had to clear away this morning, mother!"

"Well! Never mind so long as you are come," said Mrs. Cratchit. "Sit ye down before the fire, my dear, and have a warm, Lord bless ye!"

"No, no! There's father coming," cried the two young Cratchits, who were everywhere at once. "Hide, Martha, hide!"

So Martha hid herself, and in came little Bob, the father, with at least three feet of comforter exclusive of the fringe, hanging down before him; and his threadbare clothes darned up and brushed, to look seasonable; and Tiny Tim upon his shoulder. Alas for Tiny Tim, he bore a little crutch, and had his limbs supported by an iron frame!

"Why, where's our Martha?" cried Bob Cratchit, looking round.

"Not coming," said Mrs. Cratchit.

"Not coming!" said Bob, with a sudden declension in his high spirits; for he had been Tim's blood horse all the way from church, and had come home rampant. "Not coming upon Christmas Day!"

Martha didn't like to see him disappointed, if it were only in joke; so she came out prematurely from behind the closet door, and ran into his arms, while the two young Cratchits hustled Tiny Tim, and bore him off into the wash-house, that he might hear the pudding singing in the copper.

"And how did little Tim behave?" asked Mrs. Cratchit, when she had rallied Bob on his credulity, and Bob had hugged his daughter to his heart's content.

"As good as gold," said Bob, "and better. Somehow he gets thoughtful, sitting by himself so much, and thinks the strangest things you ever heard. He told me, coming home, that he hoped the people saw him in the church, because he was a cripple, and it might be pleasant to them to remember upon Christmas Day, who made lame beggars walk, and blind men see."

Bob's voice was tremulous when he told them this, and trembled more when he said that Tiny Tim was growing strong and hearty.

His active little crutch was heard upon the floor, and back came Tiny Tim before another word was spoken, escorted by his brother and sister to his stool before the fire; and while Bob, turning up his cuffs—as if, poor fellow, they were capable of being made more shabby—compounded some hot mixture in a jug with gin and lemons, and stirred it round and round and put it on the hob to simmer; Master Peter, and the two ubiquitous young Cratchits went to fetch the goose, with which they soon returned in high procession.

Such a bustle ensued that you might have thought a goose the rarest of all birds; a feathered phenomenon, to which a black swan was a matter of course—and in truth it was something very like it in that house. Mrs. Cratchit made the gravy (ready beforehand in a little saucepan) hissing hot; Master Peter mashed the potatoes with incredible vigour; Miss Belinda sweetened up the apple-sauce; Martha dusted the hot plates; Bob took Tiny Tim beside him in a tiny corner at the table; the two young Cratchits set chairs for everybody, not forgetting themselves, and mounting guard upon their posts, crammed spoons into their mouths, lest they should shriek for goose before their turn came to be helped. At last the dishes were set on, and grace was said. It was succeeded by a breathless pause, as Mrs. Cratchit, looking slowly all along the carving-knife, prepared to plunge it in the breast; but when she did, and when the long expected gush of stuffing issued forth, one murmur of delight arose all round the board, and even Tiny Tim, excited by the two young Cratchits, beat on the table with the handle of his knife, and feebly cried Hurrah!

There never was such a goose. Bob said he didn't believe there ever was such a goose cooked. Its tenderness and flavour, size and cheapness, were the themes of universal admiration. Eked out by apple-sauce and mashed potatoes, it was a sufficient dinner for the whole family; indeed, as Mrs. Cratchit said with great delight (surveying one small atom of a bone upon the dish), they hadn't ate it all at last! Yet every one had had enough, and the youngest Cratchits in particular, were steeped in sage and onion to the eyebrows! But now, the plates being changed by Miss Belinda, Mrs. Cratchit left the room alone–too nervous to bear witnesses–to take the pudding up and bring it in.

Suppose it should not be done enough! Suppose it should break in turning out! Suppose somebody should have got over the wall of the back-yard, and stolen it, while they were merry with the goose–a supposition at which the two young Cratchits became livid! All sorts of horrors were supposed.

Hallo! A great deal of steam! The pudding was out of the copper. A smell like a washing-day! That was the cloth. A smell like an eating-house and a pastrycook's next door to each other, with a laundress's next door to that! That was the pudding! In half a minute Mrs. Cratchit entered–flushed, but smiling proudly—with the pudding, like a speckled cannon-ball, so hard and firm, blazing in half of half-a-quartern of ignited brandy, and bedight with Christmas holly stuck into the top.

Oh, a wonderful pudding! Bob Cratchit said, and calmly too, that he regarded it as the greatest success achieved by Mrs. Cratchit since their marriage. Mrs. Cratchit said that now the weight was off her mind, she would confess she had had her doubts about the quantity of flour. Everybody had something to say about it, but nobody said or thought it was at all a small pudding for a large family. It would have been flat heresy to do so. Any Cratchit would have blushed to hint at such a thing.

At last the dinner was all done, the cloth was cleared, the hearth swept, and the fire made up. The compound in the jug being tasted, and considered perfect, apples and oranges were put upon the table, and a shovel-full of chestnuts on the fire. Then all the Cratchit family drew round the hearth, in what Bob Cratchit called a circle, meaning half a one; and at Bob Cratchit's elbow stood the family display of glass. Two tumblers, and a custard-cup without a handle.

These held the hot stuff from the jug, however, as well as golden goblets would have done; and Bob served it out with beaming looks, while the chestnuts on the fire sputtered and cracked noisily. Then Bob proposed:

"A Merry Christmas to us all, my dears. God bless us!"

Which all the family re-echoed.

"God bless us every one!" said Tiny Tim, the last of all.

He sat very close to his father's side upon his little stool. Bob held his withered little hand in his, as if he loved the child, and wished to keep him by his side, and dreaded that he might be taken from him.

"Spirit," said Scrooge, with an interest he had never felt before, "tell me if Tiny Tim will live."

"I see a vacant seat," replied the Ghost, "in the poor chimney-corner, and a crutch without an owner, carefully preserved. If these shadows remain unaltered by the Future, the child will die."

"No, no," said Scrooge. "Oh, no, kind Spirit! say he will be spared."

"If these shadows remain unaltered by the Future, none other of my race," returned the Ghost, "will find him here. What then? If he be like to die, he had better do it, and decrease the surplus population."

Scrooge hung his head to hear his own words quoted by the Spirit, and was overcome with penitence and grief.

"Man," said the Ghost, "if man you be in heart, not adamant, forbear that wicked cant until you have discovered What the surplus is, and Where it is. Will you decide what men shall live, what men shall die? It may be, that in the sight of Heaven, you are more worthless and less fit to live than millions like this poor man's child. Oh God! to hear the Insect on the leaf pronouncing on the too much life among his hungry brothers in the dust!"

Scrooge bent before the Ghost's rebuke, and trembling cast his eyes upon the ground. But he raised them speedily, on hearing his own name.

"Mr. Scrooge!" said Bob; "I'll give you Mr. Scrooge, the Founder of the Feast!"

"The Founder of the Feast indeed!" cried Mrs. Cratchit, reddening. "I wish I had him here. I'd give him a piece of my mind to feast upon, and I hope he'd have a good appetite for it."

"My dear," said Bob, "the children! Christmas Day."

"It should be Christmas Day, I am sure," said she, "on which one drinks the health of such an odious, stingy, hard, unfeeling man as Mr. Scrooge. You know he is, Robert! Nobody knows it better than you do, poor fellow!"

"My dear," was Bob's mild answer, "Christmas Day."

"I'll drink his health for your sake and the Day's," said Mrs. Cratchit, "not for his. Long life to him! A merry Christmas and a happy new year! He'll be very merry and very happy, I have no doubt!"

The children drank the toast after her. It was the first of their proceedings which had no heartiness. Tiny Tim drank it last of all, but he didn't care twopence for it. Scrooge was the Ogre of the family. The mention of his name cast a dark shadow on the party, which was not dispelled for full five minutes.

After it had passed away, they were ten times merrier than before, from the mere relief of Scrooge the Baleful being done with. Bob Cratchit told them how he had a situation in his eye for Master Peter, which would bring in, if obtained, full five-and-sixpence weekly. The two young Cratchits laughed tremendously at the idea of Peter's being a man of business; and Peter himself looked thoughtfully at the fire from between his collars, as if he were deliberating what particular investments he should favour when he came into the receipt of that bewildering income. Martha, who was a poor apprentice at a milliner's, then told them what kind of work she had to do, and how many hours she worked at a stretch, and how she meant to lie abed to-morrow morning for a good long rest; to-morrow being a holiday she passed at home. Also how she had seen a countess and a lord some days before, and how the lord "was much about as tall as Peter;" at which Peter pulled up his collars so high that you couldn't have seen his head if you had been there. All this time the chestnuts and the jug went round and round; and by-and-bye they had a song, about a lost child travelling in the snow, from Tiny Tim, who had a plaintive little voice, and sang it very well indeed.

There was nothing of high mark in this. They were not a handsome family; they were not well dressed; their shoes were far from being water-proof; their clothes were scanty; and Peter might have known, and very likely did, the inside of a pawnbroker's. But, they were happy, grateful, pleased with one another, and contented with the time; and when they faded, and looked happier yet in the bright sprinklings of the Spirit's torch at parting, Scrooge had his eye upon them, and especially on Tiny Tim, until the last.

By this time it was getting dark, and snowing pretty heavily; and as Scrooge and the Spirit went along the streets, the brightness of the roaring fires in kitchens, parlours, and all sorts of rooms, was wonderful. Here, the flickering of the blaze showed preparations for a cosy dinner, with hot plates baking through and through before the fire, and deep red curtains, ready to be drawn to shut out cold and darkness. There all the children of the house were running out into the snow to meet their married sisters, brothers, cousins, uncles, aunts, and be the first to greet them. Here, again, were shadows on the window-blind of guests assembling; and there a group of handsome girls, all hooded and fur-booted, and all chattering at once, tripped lightly off to some near neighbour's house; where, woe upon the single man who saw them enter–artful witches, well they knew it–in a glow!

But, if you had judged from the numbers of people on their way to friendly gatherings, you might have thought that no one was at home to give them welcome when they got there, instead of every house expecting company, and piling up its fires half-chimney high. Blessings on it, how the Ghost exulted! How it bared its breadth of breast, and opened its capacious palm, and floated on, outpouring, with a generous hand, its bright and harmless mirth on everything within its reach! The very lamplighter, who ran on before, dotting the dusky street with specks of light, and who was dressed to spend the evening somewhere, laughed out loudly as the Spirit passed, though little kenned the lamplighter that he had any company but Christmas!

And now, without a word of warning from the Ghost, they stood upon a bleak and desert moor, where monstrous masses of rude stone were cast about, as though it were the burial-place of giants; and water spread itself wheresoever it listed, or would have done so, but for the frost that held it prisoner; and nothing grew but moss and furze, and coarse rank grass. Down in the west the setting sun had left a streak of fiery red, which glared upon the desolation for an instant, like a sullen eye, and frowning lower, lower, lower yet, was lost in the thick gloom of darkest night.

"What place is this?" asked Scrooge.

"A place where Miners live, who labour in the bowels of the earth," returned the Spirit. "But they know me. See!"

A light shone from the window of a hut, and swiftly they advanced towards it. Passing through the wall of mud and stone, they found a cheerful company assembled round a glowing fire. An old, old man and woman, with their children and their children's children, and another generation beyond that, all decked out gaily in their holiday attire. The old man, in a voice that seldom rose above the howling of the wind upon the barren waste, was singing them a Christmas song—it had been a very old song when he was a boy—and from time to time they all joined in the chorus. So surely as they raised their voices, the old man got quite blithe and loud; and so surely as they stopped, his vigour sank again.

The Spirit did not tarry here, but bade Scrooge hold his robe, and passing on above the moor, sped—whither? Not to sea? To sea. To Scrooge's horror, looking back, he saw the last of the land, a frightful range of rocks, behind them; and his ears were deafened by the thundering of water, as it rolled and roared, and raged among the dreadful caverns it had worn, and fiercely tried to undermine the earth.

Built upon a dismal reef of sunken rocks, some league or so from shore, on which the waters chafed and dashed, the wild year through, there stood a solitary lighthouse. Great heaps of sea-weed clung to its base, and storm-birds —born of the wind one might suppose, as sea-weed of the water—rose and fell about it, like the waves they skimmed.

But even here, two men who watched the light had made

a fire, that through the loophole in the thick stone wall shed out a ray of brightness on the awful sea. Joining their horny hands over the rough table at which they sat, they wished each other Merry Christmas in their can of grog; and one of them: the elder, too, with his face all damaged and scarred with hard weather, as the figure-head of an old ship might be: struck up a sturdy song that was like a Gale in itself.

Again the Ghost sped on, above the black and heaving sea —on, on—until, being far away, as he told Scrooge, from any shore, they lighted on a ship. They stood beside the helmsman at the wheel, the look-out in the bow, the officers who had the watch; dark, ghostly figures in their several stations; but every man among them hummed a Christmas tune, or had a Christmas thought, or spoke below his breath to his companion of some bygone Christmas Day, with homeward hopes belonging to it. And every man on board, waking or sleeping, good or bad, had had a kinder word for another on that day than on any day in the year; and had shared to some extent in its festivities; and had remembered those he cared for at a distance, and had known that they delighted to remember him.

It was a great surprise to Scrooge, while listening to the moaning of the wind, and thinking what a solemn thing it was to move on through the lonely darkness over an unknown abyss, whose depths were secrets as profound as Death: it was a great surprise to Scrooge, while thus engaged, to hear a hearty laugh. It was a much greater surprise to Scrooge to recognise it as his own nephew's and to find himself in a bright, dry, gleaming room, with the Spirit standing smiling by his side, and looking at that same nephew with approving affability!

"Ha, ha!" laughed Scrooge's nephew. "Ha, ha, ha!"

If you should happen, by any unlikely chance, to know a man more blest in a laugh than Scrooge's nephew, all I can say is, I should like to know him too. Introduce him to me, and I'll cultivate his acquaintance.

It is a fair, even-handed, noble adjustment of things, that while there is infection in disease and sorrow, there is nothing in the world so irresistibly contagious as laughter and good-humour. When Scrooge's nephew laughed in this way: holding his sides, rolling his head, and twisting his face into the most extravagant contortions: Scrooge's niece, by marriage, laughed as heartily as he. And their assembled friends being not a bit behindhand, roared out lustily.

"Ha, ha! Ha, ha, ha, ha!"

"He said that Christmas was a humbug, as I live!" cried Scrooge's nephew. "He believed it too!"

"More shame for him, Fred!" said Scrooge's niece, indignantly. Bless those women; they never do anything by halves. They are always in earnest.

She was very pretty: exceedingly pretty. With a dimpled, surprised-looking, capital face; a ripe little mouth, that seemed made to be kissed—as no doubt it was; all kinds of good little dots about her chin, that melted into one another when she laughed; and the sunniest pair of eyes you ever saw in any little creature's head. Altogether she was what you would have called provoking, you know; but satisfactory, too. Oh, perfectly satisfactory.

"He's a comical old fellow," said Scrooge's nephew, "that's the truth: and not so pleasant as he might be. However, his offences carry their own punishment, and I have nothing to say against him."

"I'm sure he is very rich, Fred," hinted Scrooge's niece. "At least you always tell me so."

"What of that, my dear!" said Scrooge's nephew. "His wealth is of no use to him. He don't do any good with it. He don't make himself comfortable with it. He hasn't the satisfaction of thinking—ha, ha, ha!—that he is ever going to benefit US with it."

"I have no patience with him," observed Scrooge's niece. Scrooge's niece's sisters, and all the other ladies, expressed the same opinion.

"Oh, I have!" said Scrooge's nephew. "I am sorry for him; I couldn't be angry with him if I tried. Who suffers by his ill whims! Himself, always. Here, he takes it into his head to dislike us, and he won't come and dine with us. What's the consequence? He don't lose much of a dinner."

"Indeed, I think he loses a very good dinner," interrupted Scrooge's niece. Everybody else said the same, and they must be allowed to have been competent judges, because they had just had dinner; and, with the dessert upon the table, were clustered round the fire, by lamplight.

"Well! I'm very glad to hear it," said Scrooge's nephew, "because I haven't great faith in these young housekeepers. What do you say, Topper?"

Topper had clearly got his eye upon one of Scrooge's niece's sisters, for he answered that a bachelor was a wretched outcast, who had no right to express an opinion on the subject. Whereat Scrooge's niece's sister—the plump one with the lace tucker: not the one with the roses—blushed.

"Do go on, Fred," said Scrooge's niece, clapping her hands. "He never finishes what he begins to say! He is such a ridiculous fellow!"

Scrooge's nephew revelled in another laugh, and as it was impossible to keep the infection off; though the plump sister tried hard to do it with aromatic vinegar; his example was unanimously followed.

"I was only going to say," said Scrooge's nephew, "that the consequence of his taking a dislike to us, and not making merry with us, is, as I think, that he loses some pleasant moments, which could do him no harm. I am sure he loses pleasanter companions than he can find in his own thoughts, either in his mouldy old office, or his dusty chambers. I mean to give him the same chance every year, whether he likes it or not, for I pity him. He may rail at Christmas till he dies, but he can't help thinking better of it—I defy him—if he finds me going there, in good temper, year after year, and saying Uncle Scrooge, how are you? If it only puts him in the vein to leave his poor clerk fifty pounds, that's something; and I think I shook him yesterday."

It was their turn to laugh now at the notion of his shaking Scrooge. But being thoroughly good-natured, and not much caring what they laughed at, so that they laughed at any rate, he encouraged them in their merriment, and passed the bottle joyously.

After tea, they had some music. For they were a musical family, and knew what they were about, when they sung a Glee or Catch, I can assure you: especially Topper, who could growl away in the bass like a good one, and never swell the large veins in his forehead, or get red in the face over it. Scrooge's niece played well upon the harp; and played among other tunes a simple little air (a mere nothing: you might learn to whistle it in two minutes), which had been familiar to the child who fetched Scrooge from the boarding-school, as he had been reminded by the Ghost of Christmas Past. When this strain of music sounded, all the things that Ghost had shown him, came upon his mind; he softened more and more; and thought that if he could have listened to it often, years ago, he might have cultivated the kindnesses of life for his own happiness with his own hands, without resorting to the sexton's spade that buried Jacob Marley.

But they didn't devote the whole evening to music. After a while they played at forfeits; for it is good to be children sometimes, and never better than at Christmas, when its mighty Founder was a child himself. Stop! There was first a game at blind-man's buff. Of course there was. And I no more believe Topper was really blind than I believe he had eyes in his boots. My opinion is, that it was a done thing between him and Scrooge's nephew; and that the Ghost of Christmas Present knew it. The way he went after that plump sister in the lace tucker, was an outrage on the credulity of human nature. Knocking down the fire-irons, tumbling over the chairs, bumping against the piano, smothering himself among the curtains, wherever she went, there went he! He always knew where the plump sister was. He wouldn't catch anybody else. If you had fallen up against him (as some of them did), on purpose, he would have made a feint of endeavouring to seize you, which would have been an affront to your understanding, and would instantly have sidled off in the direction of the plump sister. She often cried out that it wasn't fair; and it really was not. But when at last, he caught her; when, in spite of all her silken rustlings, and her rapid flutterings past him, he got her into a corner whence there was no escape; then his conduct was the most execrable. For his pretending not to know her; his pretending that it was necessary to touch her head-dress, and further to assure himself of her identity by pressing a certain ring upon her finger, and a certain chain about her neck; was vile, monstrous! No doubt she told him her opinion of it, when, another blind-man being in office, they were so very confidential together, behind the curtains.

Scrooge's niece was not one of the blind-man's buff party, but was made comfortable with a large chair and a footstool, in a snug corner, where the Ghost and Scrooge were close behind her. But she joined in the forfeits, and loved her love to admiration with all the letters of the alphabet. Likewise at the game of How, When, and Where, she was very great, and to the secret joy of Scrooge's nephew, beat her sisters hollow: though they were sharp girls too, as Topper could have told you. There might have been twenty people there, young and old, but they all played, and so did Scrooge; for wholly forgetting in the interest he had in what was going on, that his voice made no sound in their ears, he sometimes came out with his guess quite loud, and very often guessed quite right, too; for the sharpest needle, best Whitechapel, warranted not to cut in the eye, was not sharper than Scrooge; blunt as he took it in his head to be.

The Ghost was greatly pleased to find him in this mood, and looked upon him with such favour, that he begged like a boy to be allowed to stay until the guests departed. But this the Spirit said could not be done.

"Here is a new game," said Scrooge. "One half hour, Spirit, only one!"

It was a Game called Yes and No, where Scrooge's nephew had to think of something, and the rest must find out what; he only answering to their questions yes or no, as the case was. The brisk fire of questioning to which he was exposed, elicited from him that he was thinking of an animal, a live animal, rather a disagreeable animal, a savage animal, an animal that growled and grunted sometimes, and talked sometimes, and lived in London, and walked about the streets, and wasn't made a show of, and wasn't led by anybody, and didn't live in a menagerie, and was never killed in a market, and was not a horse, or an ass, or a cow, or a bull, or a tiger, or a dog, or a pig, or a cat, or a bear. At every fresh question that was put to him, this nephew burst into a fresh roar of laughter; and was so inexpressibly tickled, that he was obliged to get up off the sofa and stamp. At last the plump sister, falling into a similar state, cried out:

"I have found it out! I know what it is, Fred! I know what it is!"

"What is it?" cried Fred.

"It's your Uncle Scro-o-o-o-oge!"

Which it certainly was. Admiration was the universal sentiment, though some objected that the reply to "Is it a bear?" ought to have been "Yes;" inasmuch as an answer in the negative was sufficient to have diverted their thoughts from Mr. Scrooge, supposing they had ever had any tendency that way.

"He has given us plenty of merriment, I am sure," said Fred, "and it would be ungrateful not to drink his health. Here is a glass of mulled wine ready to our hand at the moment; and I say, 'Uncle Scrooge!'"

"Well! Uncle Scrooge!" they cried.

"A Merry Christmas and a Happy New Year to the old man, whatever he is!" said Scrooge's nephew. "He wouldn't take it from me, but may he have it, nevertheless. Uncle Scrooge!"

Uncle Scrooge had imperceptibly become so gay and light of heart, that he would have pledged the unconscious company in return, and thanked them in an inaudible speech, if the Ghost had given him time. But the whole scene passed off in the breath of the last word spoken by his nephew; and he and the Spirit were again upon their travels.

Much they saw, and far they went, and many homes they visited, but always with a happy end. The Spirit stood beside sick beds, and they were cheerful; on foreign lands, and they were close at home; by struggling men, and they were patient in their greater hope; by poverty, and it was rich. In almshouse, hospital, and jail, in misery's every refuge, where vain man in his little brief authority had not made fast the door, and barred the Spirit out, he left his blessing, and taught Scrooge his precepts.

It was a long night, if it were only a night; but Scrooge had his doubts of this, because the Christmas Holidays appeared to be condensed into the space of time they passed together. It was strange, too, that while Scrooge remained unaltered in his outward form, the Ghost grew older, clearly older. Scrooge had observed this change, but never spoke of it, until they left a children's Twelfth Night party, when, looking at the Spirit as they stood together in an open place, he noticed that its hair was grey.

"Are spirits' lives so short?" asked Scrooge.

"My life upon this globe, is very brief," replied the Ghost. "It ends to-night."

"To-night!" cried Scrooge.

"To-night at midnight. Hark! The time is drawing near."

The chimes were ringing the three quarters past eleven at that moment.

"Forgive me if I am not justified in what I ask," said Scrooge, looking intently at the Spirit's robe, "but I see something strange, and not belonging to yourself, protruding from your skirts. Is it a foot or a claw?"

"It might be a claw, for the flesh there is upon it," was the Spirit's sorrowful reply. "Look here."

From the foldings of its robe, it brought two children; wretched, abject, frightful, hideous, miserable. They knelt down at its feet, and clung upon the outside of its garment.

"Oh, Man! look here. Look, look, down here!" exclaimed the Ghost.

They were a boy and girl. Yellow, meagre, ragged, scowling, wolfish; but prostrate, too, in their humility. Where graceful youth should have filled their features out, and touched them with its freshest tints, a stale and shrivelled hand, like that of age, had pinched, and twisted them, and pulled them into shreds. Where angels might have sat enthroned, devils lurked, and glared out menacing. No change, no degradation, no perversion of humanity, in any grade, through all the mysteries of wonderful creation, has monsters half so horrible and dread.

Scrooge started back, appalled. Having them shown to him in this way, he tried to say they were fine children, but the words choked themselves, rather than be parties to a lie of such enormous magnitude.

"Spirit! are they yours?" Scrooge could say no more.

"They are Man's," said the Spirit, looking down upon them. "And they cling to me, appealing from their fathers. This boy is Ignorance. This girl is Want. Beware them both, and all of their degree, but most of all beware this boy, for on his brow I see that written which is Doom, unless the writing be erased. Deny it!" cried the Spirit, stretching out its hand towards the city. "Slander those who tell it ye! Admit it for your factious purposes, and make it worse. And bide the end!"

"Have they no refuge or resource?" cried Scrooge.

"Are there no prisons?" said the Spirit, turning on him for the last time with his own words. "Are there no workhouses?"

The bell struck twelve.

Scrooge looked about him for the Ghost, and saw it not. As the last stroke ceased to vibrate, he remembered the prediction of old Jacob Marley, and lifting up his eyes, beheld a solemn Phantom, draped and hooded, coming, like a mist along the ground, towards him.

STAVE IV: THE LAST OF
THE SPIRITS

THE Phantom slowly, gravely, silently, approached. When it came near him, Scrooge bent down upon his knee; for in the very air through which this Spirit moved it seemed to scatter gloom and mystery.

It was shrouded in a deep black garment, which concealed its head, its face, its form, and left nothing of it visible save one outstretched hand. But for this it would have been difficult to detach its figure from the night, and separate it from the darkness by which it was surrounded.

He felt that it was tall and stately when it came beside him, and that its mysterious presence filled him with a solemn dread. He knew no more, for the Spirit neither spoke nor moved.

"I am in the presence of the Ghost of Christmas Yet To Come?" said Scrooge.

The Spirit answered not, but pointed onward with its hand.

"You are about to show me shadows of the things that have

not happened, but will happen in the time before us," Scrooge pursued. "Is that so, Spirit?"

The upper portion of the garment was contracted for an instant in its folds, as if the Spirit had inclined its head. That was the only answer he received.

Although well used to ghostly company by this time, Scrooge feared the silent shape so much that his legs trembled beneath him, and he found that he could hardly stand when he prepared to follow it. The Spirit paused a moment, as observing his condition, and giving him time to recover.

But Scrooge was all the worse for this. It thrilled him with a vague uncertain horror, to know that behind the dusky shroud, there were ghostly eyes intently fixed upon him, while he, though he stretched his own to the utmost, could see nothing but a spectral hand and one great heap of black.

"Ghost of the Future!" he exclaimed, "I fear you more than any spectre I have seen. But as I know your purpose is to do me good, and as I hope to live to be another man from what I was, I am prepared to bear you company, and do it with a thankful heart. Will you not speak to me?"

It gave him no reply. The hand was pointed straight before them.

"Lead on!" said Scrooge. "Lead on! The night is waning fast, and it is precious time to me, I know. Lead on, Spirit!"

The Phantom moved away as it had come towards him. Scrooge followed in the shadow of its dress, which bore him up, he thought, and carried him along.

They scarcely seemed to enter the city; for the city rather seemed to spring up about them, and encompass them of its

own act. But there they were, in the heart of it; on 'Change,
amongst the merchants; who hurried up and down, and
chinked the money in their pockets, and conversed in groups,
and looked at their watches, and trifled thoughtfully with their
great gold seals; and so forth, as Scrooge had seen them often.

The Spirit stopped beside one little knot of business
men. Observing that the hand was pointed to them, Scrooge
advanced to listen to their talk.

"No," said a great fat man with a monstrous chin, "I don't
know much about it, either way. I only know he's dead."

"When did he die?" inquired another.

"Last night, I believe."

"Why, what was the matter with him?" asked a third, taking
a vast quantity of snuff out of a very large snuff-box. "I thought
he'd never die."

"God knows," said the first, with a yawn.

"What has he done with his money?" asked a red-faced
gentleman with a pendulous excrescence on the end of his
nose, that shook like the gills of a turkey-cock.

"I haven't heard," said the man with the large chin, yawning
again. "Left it to his company, perhaps. He hasn't left it to me.
That's all I know."

This pleasantry was received with a general laugh.

"It's likely to be a very cheap funeral," said the same speaker;
"for upon my life I don't know of anybody to go to it. Suppose
we make up a party and volunteer?"

"I don't mind going if a lunch is provided," observed the
gentleman with the excrescence on his nose. "But I must be
fed, if I make one."

Another laugh.

"Well, I am the most disinterested among you, after all," said the first speaker, "for I never wear black gloves, and I never eat lunch. But I'll offer to go, if anybody else will. When I come to think of it, I'm not at all sure that I wasn't his most particular friend; for we used to stop and speak whenever we met. Bye, bye!"

Speakers and listeners strolled away, and mixed with other groups. Scrooge knew the men, and looked towards the Spirit for an explanation.

The Phantom glided on into a street. Its finger pointed to two persons meeting. Scrooge listened again, thinking that the explanation might lie here.

He knew these men, also, perfectly. They were men of business: very wealthy, and of great importance. He had made a point always of standing well in their esteem: in a business point of view, that is; strictly in a business point of view.

"How are you?" said one.

"How are you?" returned the other.

"Well!" said the first. "Old Scratch has got his own at last, hey?"

"So I am told," returned the second. "Cold, isn't it?"

"Seasonable for Christmas time. You're not a skater, I suppose?"

"No. No. Something else to think of. Good morning!"

Not another word. That was their meeting, their conversation, and their parting.

Scrooge was at first inclined to be surprised that the Spirit should attach importance to conversations apparently so trivial;

but feeling assured that they must have some hidden purpose,
he set himself to consider what it was likely to be. They could
scarcely be supposed to have any bearing on the death of Jacob,
his old partner, for that was Past, and this Ghost's province
was the Future. Nor could he think of any one immediately
connected with himself, to whom he could apply them. But
nothing doubting that to whomsoever they applied they had
some latent moral for his own improvement, he resolved to
treasure up every word he heard, and everything he saw; and
especially to observe the shadow of himself when it appeared.
For he had an expectation that the conduct of his future self
would give him the clue he missed, and would render the solu-
tion of these riddles easy.

He looked about in that very place for his own image; but
another man stood in his accustomed corner, and though the
clock pointed to his usual time of day for being there, he saw
no likeness of himself among the multitudes that poured in
through the Porch. It gave him little surprise, however; for he
had been revolving in his mind a change of life, and thought
and hoped he saw his new-born resolutions carried out in this.

Quiet and dark, beside him stood the Phantom, with its outstretched hand. When he roused himself from his thoughtful
quest, he fancied from the turn of the hand, and its situation in
reference to himself, that the Unseen Eyes were looking at him
keenly. It made him shudder, and feel very cold.

They left the busy scene, and went into an obscure part of
the town, where Scrooge had never penetrated before, although
he recognised its situation, and its bad repute. The ways were
foul and narrow; the shops and houses wretched; the people

half-naked, drunken, slipshod, ugly. Alleys and archways, like so many cesspools, disgorged their offences of smell, and dirt, and life, upon the straggling streets; and the whole quarter reeked with crime, with filth, and misery.

Far in this den of infamous resort, there was a low-browed, beetling shop, below a pent-house roof, where iron, old rags, bottles, bones, and greasy offal, were bought. Upon the floor within, were piled up heaps of rusty keys, nails, chains, hinges, files, scales, weights, and refuse iron of all kinds. Secrets that few would like to scrutinise were bred and hidden in mountains of unseemly rags, masses of corrupted fat, and sepulchres of bones. Sitting in among the wares he dealt in, by a charcoal stove, made of old bricks, was a grey-haired rascal, nearly seventy years of age; who had screened himself from the cold air without, by a frousy curtaining of miscellaneous tatters, hung upon a line; and smoked his pipe in all the luxury of calm retirement.

Scrooge and the Phantom came into the presence of this man, just as a woman with a heavy bundle slunk into the shop. But she had scarcely entered, when another woman, similarly laden, came in too; and she was closely followed by a man in faded black, who was no less startled by the sight of them, than they had been upon the recognition of each other. After a short period of blank astonishment, in which the old man with the pipe had joined them, they all three burst into a laugh.

"Let the charwoman alone to be the first!" cried she who had entered first. "Let the laundress alone to be the second; and let the undertaker's man alone to be the third. Look here, old Joe, here's a chance! If we haven't all three met here without meaning it!"

"You couldn't have met in a better place," said old Joe, removing his pipe from his mouth. "Come into the parlour. You were made free of it long ago, you know; and the other two an't strangers. Stop till I shut the door of the shop. Ah! How it skreeks! There an't such a rusty bit of metal in the place as its own hinges, I believe; and I'm sure there's no such old bones here, as mine. Ha, ha! We're all suitable to our calling, we're well matched. Come into the parlour. Come into the parlour."

The parlour was the space behind the screen of rags. The old man raked the fire together with an old stair-rod, and having trimmed his smoky lamp (for it was night), with the stem of his pipe, put it in his mouth again.

While he did this, the woman who had already spoken threw her bundle on the floor, and sat down in a flaunting manner on a stool; crossing her elbows on her knees, and looking with a bold defiance at the other two.

"What odds then! What odds, Mrs. Dilber?" said the woman. "Every person has a right to take care of themselves. He always did."

"That's true, indeed!" said the laundress. "No man more so."

"Why then, don't stand staring as if you was afraid, woman; who's the wiser? We're not going to pick holes in each other's coats, I suppose?"

"No, indeed!" said Mrs. Dilber and the man together. "We should hope not."

"Very well, then!" cried the woman. "That's enough. Who's the worse for the loss of a few things like these? Not a dead man, I suppose."

"No, indeed," said Mrs. Dilber, laughing.

"If he wanted to keep 'em after he was dead, a wicked old screw," pursued the woman, "why wasn't he natural in his lifetime? If he had been, he'd have had somebody to look after him when he was struck with Death, instead of lying gasping out his last there, alone by himself."

"It's the truest word that ever was spoke," said Mrs. Dilber. "It's a judgment on him."

"I wish it was a little heavier judgment," replied the woman; "and it should have been, you may depend upon it, if I could have laid my hands on anything else. Open that bundle, old Joe, and let me know the value of it. Speak out plain. I'm not afraid to be the first, nor afraid for them to see it. We know pretty well that we were helping ourselves, before we met here, I believe. It's no sin. Open the bundle, Joe."

But the gallantry of her friends would not allow of this; and the man in faded black, mounting the breach first, produced his plunder. It was not extensive. A seal or two, a pencil-case, a pair of sleeve-buttons, and a brooch of no great value, were all. They were severally examined and appraised by old Joe, who chalked the sums he was disposed to give for each, upon the wall, and added them up into a total when he found there was nothing more to come.

"That's your account," said Joe, "and I wouldn't give another sixpence, if I was to be boiled for not doing it. Who's next?"

Mrs. Dilber was next. Sheets and towels, a little wearing apparel, two old-fashioned silver teaspoons, a pair of sugar-tongs, and a few boots. Her account was stated on the wall in the same manner.

"I always give too much to ladies. It's a weakness of mine, and that's the way I ruin myself," said old Joe. "That's your account. If you asked me for another penny, and made it an open question, I'd repent of being so liberal and knock off half-a-crown."

"And now undo my bundle, Joe," said the first woman.

Joe went down on his knees for the greater convenience of opening it, and having unfastened a great many knots, dragged out a large and heavy roll of some dark stuff.

"What do you call this?" said Joe. "Bed-curtains!"

"Ah!" returned the woman, laughing and leaning forward on her crossed arms. "Bed-curtains!"

"You don't mean to say you took 'em down, rings and all, with him lying there?" said Joe.

"Yes I do," replied the woman. "Why not?"

"You were born to make your fortune," said Joe, "and you'll certainly do it."

"I certainly shan't hold my hand, when I can get anything in it by reaching it out, for the sake of such a man as He was, I promise you, Joe," returned the woman coolly. "Don't drop that oil upon the blankets, now."

"His blankets?" asked Joe.

"Whose else's do you think?" replied the woman. "He isn't likely to take cold without 'em, I dare say."

"I hope he didn't die of anything catching? Eh?" said old Joe, stopping in his work, and looking up.

"Don't you be afraid of that," returned the woman. "I an't so fond of his company that I'd loiter about him for such things, if he did. Ah! you may look through that shirt till your eyes ache; but you won't find a hole in it, nor a threadbare place. It's the best he had, and a fine one too. They'd have wasted it, if it hadn't been for me."

"What do you call wasting of it?" asked old Joe.

"Putting it on him to be buried in, to be sure," replied the woman with a laugh. "Somebody was fool enough to do it, but I took it off again. If calico an't good enough for such a purpose, it isn't good enough for anything. It's quite as becoming to the body. He can't look uglier than he did in that one."

Scrooge listened to this dialogue in horror. As they sat grouped about their spoil, in the scanty light afforded by the old man's lamp, he viewed them with a detestation and disgust, which could hardly have been greater, though they had been obscene demons, marketing the corpse itself.

"Ha, ha!" laughed the same woman, when old Joe, producing a flannel bag with money in it, told out their several gains upon the ground. "This is the end of it, you see! He frightened every one away from him when he was alive, to profit us when he was dead! Ha, ha, ha!"

"Spirit!" said Scrooge, shuddering from head to foot. "I see, I see. The case of this unhappy man might be my own. My life tends that way, now. Merciful Heaven, what is this!"

He recoiled in terror, for the scene had changed, and now he almost touched a bed: a bare, uncurtained bed: on which, beneath a ragged sheet, there lay a something covered up, which, though it was dumb, announced itself in awful language.

The room was very dark, too dark to be observed with any accuracy, though Scrooge glanced round it in obedience to a secret impulse, anxious to know what kind of room it was. A pale light, rising in the outer air, fell straight upon the bed; and on it, plundered and bereft, unwatched, unwept, uncared for, was the body of this man.

Scrooge glanced towards the Phantom. Its steady hand was pointed to the head. The cover was so carelessly adjusted that the slightest raising of it, the motion of a finger upon Scrooge's part, would have disclosed the face. He thought of it, felt how easy it would be to do, and longed to do it; but had no more power to withdraw the veil than to dismiss the spectre at his side.

Oh cold, cold, rigid, dreadful Death, set up thine altar here, and dress it with such terrors as thou hast at thy command: for this is thy dominion! But of the loved, revered, and honoured head, thou canst not turn one hair to thy dread purposes, or make one feature odious. It is not that the hand is heavy and will fall down when released; it is not that the heart and pulse are still; but that the hand WAS open, generous, and true; the heart brave, warm, and tender; and the pulse a man's. Strike, Shadow, strike! And see his good deeds springing from the wound, to sow the world with life immortal!

No voice pronounced these words in Scrooge's ears, and yet he heard them when he looked upon the bed. He thought, if this man could be raised up now, what would be his foremost thoughts? Avarice, hard-dealing, griping cares? They have brought him to a rich end, truly!

He lay, in the dark empty house, with not a man, a woman, or a child, to say that he was kind to me in this or that, and for the memory of one kind word I will be kind to him. A cat was tearing at the door, and there was a sound of gnawing rats beneath the hearth-stone. What they wanted in the room of death, and why they were so restless and disturbed, Scrooge did not dare to think.

"Spirit!" he said, "this is a fearful place. In leaving it, I shall not leave its lesson, trust me. Let us go!"

Still the Ghost pointed with an unmoved finger to the head.

"I understand you," Scrooge returned, "and I would do it, if I could. But I have not the power, Spirit. I have not the power."

Again it seemed to look upon him.

"If there is any person in the town, who feels emotion caused by this man's death," said Scrooge quite agonised, "show that person to me, Spirit, I beseech you!"

The Phantom spread its dark robe before him for a moment, like a wing; and withdrawing it, revealed a room by daylight, where a mother and her children were.

She was expecting some one, and with anxious eagerness; for she walked up and down the room; started at every sound; looked out from the window; glanced at the clock; tried, but in vain, to work with her needle; and could hardly bear the voices of the children in their play.

At length the long-expected knock was heard. She hurried to the door, and met her husband; a man whose face was careworn and depressed, though he was young. There was a remarkable expression in it now; a kind of serious delight of which he felt ashamed, and which he struggled to repress.

He sat down to the dinner that had been hoarding for him by the fire; and when she asked him faintly what news (which was not until after a long silence), he appeared embarrassed how to answer.

"Is it good?" she said, "or bad?"–to help him.

"Bad," he answered.

"We are quite ruined?"

"No. There is hope yet, Caroline."

"If he relents," she said, amazed, "there is! Nothing is past hope, if such a miracle has happened."

"He is past relenting," said her husband. "He is dead."

She was a mild and patient creature if her face spoke truth; but she was thankful in her soul to hear it, and she said so, with clasped hands. She prayed forgiveness the next moment, and was sorry; but the first was the emotion of her heart.

"What the half-drunken woman whom I told you of last night, said to me, when I tried to see him and obtain a week's delay; and what I thought was a mere excuse to avoid me; turns out to have been quite true. He was not only very ill, but dying, then."

"To whom will our debt be transferred?"

"I don't know. But before that time we shall be ready with the money; and even though we were not, it would be a bad fortune indeed to find so merciless a creditor in his successor. We may sleep to-night with light hearts, Caroline!"

Yes. Soften it as they would, their hearts were lighter. The children's faces, hushed and clustered round to hear what they so little understood, were brighter; and it was a happier house for this man's death! The only emotion that the Ghost could show him, caused by the event, was one of pleasure.

"Let me see some tenderness connected with a death," said Scrooge; "or that dark chamber, Spirit, which we left just now, will be for ever present to me."

The Ghost conducted him through several streets familiar to his feet; and as they went along, Scrooge looked here and there to find himself, but nowhere was he to be seen. They entered poor Bob Cratchit's house; the dwelling he had visited before; and found the mother and the children seated round the fire.

Quiet. Very quiet. The noisy little Cratchits were as still as statues in one corner, and sat looking up at Peter, who had a book before him. The mother and her daughters were engaged in sewing. But surely they were very quiet!

"'And He took a child, and set him in the midst of them.'"

Where had Scrooge heard those words? He had not dreamed them. The boy must have read them out, as he and the Spirit crossed the threshold. Why did he not go on?

The mother laid her work upon the table, and put her hand up to her face.

"The colour hurts my eyes," she said.

The colour? Ah, poor Tiny Tim!

"They're better now again," said Cratchit's wife. "It makes them weak by candle-light; and I wouldn't show weak eyes to your father when he comes home, for the world. It must be near his time."

"Past it rather," Peter answered, shutting up his book. "But I think he has walked a little slower than he used, these few last evenings, mother."

They were very quiet again. At last she said, and in a steady, cheerful voice, that only faltered once:

"I have known him walk with—I have known him walk with Tiny Tim upon his shoulder, very fast indeed."

"And so have I," cried Peter. "Often."

"And so have I," exclaimed another. So had all.

"But he was very light to carry," she resumed, intent upon her work, "and his father loved him so, that it was no trouble: no trouble. And there is your father at the door!"

She hurried out to meet him; and little Bob in his comforter —he had need of it, poor fellow—came in. His tea was ready for him on the hob, and they all tried who should help him to it most. Then the two young Cratchits got upon his knees and laid, each child a little cheek, against his face, as if they said, "Don't mind it, father. Don't be grieved!"

Bob was very cheerful with them, and spoke pleasantly to all the family. He looked at the work upon the table, and praised the industry and speed of Mrs. Cratchit and the girls. They would be done long before Sunday, he said.

"Sunday! You went to-day, then, Robert?" said his wife.

"Yes, my dear," returned Bob. "I wish you could have gone. It would have done you good to see how green a place it is. But you'll see it often. I promised him that I would walk there on a Sunday. My little, little child!" cried Bob. "My little child!"

He broke down all at once. He couldn't help it. If he could have helped it, he and his child would have been farther apart perhaps than they were.

He left the room, and went up-stairs into the room above, which was lighted cheerfully, and hung with Christmas. There was a chair set close beside the child, and there were signs of some one having been there, lately. Poor Bob sat down in it, and when he had thought a little and composed himself, he kissed the little face. He was reconciled to what had happened, and went down again quite happy.

They drew about the fire, and talked; the girls and mother working still. Bob told them of the extraordinary kindness of Mr. Scrooge's nephew, whom he had scarcely seen but once, and who, meeting him in the street that day, and seeing that he looked a little–"just a little down you know," said Bob, inquired what had happened to distress him. "On which," said Bob, "for he is the pleasantest-spoken gentleman you ever heard, I told him. 'I am heartily sorry for it, Mr. Cratchit,' he said, 'and heartily sorry for your good wife.' By the bye, how he ever knew that, I don't know."

"Knew what, my dear?"

"Why, that you were a good wife," replied Bob.

"Everybody knows that!" said Peter.

"Very well observed, my boy!" cried Bob. "I hope they do. 'Heartily sorry,' he said, 'for your good wife. If I can be of service to you in any way,' he said, giving me his card, 'that's where I live. Pray come to me.' Now, it wasn't," cried Bob, "for the sake of anything he might be able to do for us, so much as for his kind way, that this was quite delightful. It really seemed as if he had known our Tiny Tim, and felt with us."

"I'm sure he's a good soul!" said Mrs. Cratchit.

"You would be surer of it, my dear," returned Bob, "if you saw and spoke to him. I shouldn't be at all surprised– mark what I say!–if he got Peter a better situation."

"Only hear that, Peter," said Mrs. Cratchit.

"And then," cried one of the girls, "Peter will be keeping company with some one, and setting up for himself."

"Get along with you!" retorted Peter, grinning.

"It's just as likely as not," said Bob, "one of these days; though there's plenty of time for that, my dear. But however and whenever we part from one another, I am sure we shall none of us forget poor Tiny Tim—shall we—or this first parting that there was among us?"

"Never, father!" cried they all.

"And I know," said Bob, "I know, my dears, that when we recollect how patient and how mild he was; although he was a little, little child; we shall not quarrel easily among ourselves, and forget poor Tiny Tim in doing it."

"No, never, father!" they all cried again.

"I am very happy," said little Bob, "I am very happy!"

Mrs. Cratchit kissed him, his daughters kissed him, the two young Cratchits kissed him, and Peter and himself shook hands. Spirit of Tiny Tim, thy childish essence was from God!

"Spectre," said Scrooge, "something informs me that our parting moment is at hand. I know it, but I know not how. Tell me what man that was whom we saw lying dead?"

The Ghost of Christmas Yet To Come conveyed him, as before—though at a different time, he thought: indeed, there seemed no order in these latter visions, save that they were in the Future—into the resorts of business men, but showed him not himself. Indeed, the Spirit did not stay for anything, but went straight on, as to the end just now desired, until besought by Scrooge to tarry for a moment.

"This court," said Scrooge, "through which we hurry now, is where my place of occupation is, and has been for a length of time. I see the house. Let me behold what I shall be, in days to come!"

The Spirit stopped; the hand was pointed elsewhere.

"The house is yonder," Scrooge exclaimed. "Why do you point away?"

The inexorable finger underwent no change.

Scrooge hastened to the window of his office, and looked in. It was an office still, but not his. The furniture was not the same, and the figure in the chair was not himself. The Phantom pointed as before.

He joined it once again, and wondering why and whither he had gone, accompanied it until they reached an iron gate. He paused to look round before entering.

A churchyard. Here, then; the wretched man whose name he had now to learn, lay underneath the ground. It was a worthy place. Walled in by houses; overrun by grass and weeds, the growth of vegetation's death, not life; choked up with too much burying; fat with repleted appetite. A worthy place!

The Spirit stood among the graves, and pointed down to One. He advanced towards it trembling. The Phantom was exactly as it had been, but he dreaded that he saw new meaning in its solemn shape.

"Before I draw nearer to that stone to which you point," said Scrooge, "answer me one question. Are these the shadows of the things that Will be, or are they shadows of things that May be, only?"

Still the Ghost pointed downward to the grave by which it stood.

"Men's courses will foreshadow certain ends, to which, if persevered in, they must lead," said Scrooge. "But if the courses be departed from, the ends will change. Say it is thus with what you show me!"

The Spirit was immovable as ever.

Scrooge crept towards it, trembling as he went; and following the finger, read upon the stone of the neglected grave his own name, EBENEZER SCROOGE.

"Am I that man who lay upon the bed?" he cried, upon his knees.

The finger pointed from the grave to him, and back again.

"No, Spirit! Oh no, no!"

The finger still was there.

"Spirit!" he cried, tight clutching at its robe, "hear me! I am not the man I was. I will not be the man I must have been but for this intercourse. Why show me this, if I am past all hope!"

For the first time the hand appeared to shake.

"Good Spirit," he pursued, as down upon the ground he fell before it: "Your nature intercedes for me, and pities me. Assure me that I yet may change these shadows you have shown me, by an altered life!"

The kind hand trembled.

"I will honour Christmas in my heart, and try to keep it all the year. I will live in the Past, the Present, and the Future. The Spirits of all Three shall strive within me. I will not shut out the lessons that they teach. Oh, tell me I may sponge away the writing on this stone!"

In his agony, he caught the spectral hand. It sought to free itself, but he was strong in his entreaty, and detained it. The Spirit, stronger yet, repulsed him.

Holding up his hands in a last prayer to have his fate reversed, he saw an alteration in the Phantom's hood and dress. It shrunk, collapsed, and dwindled down into a bedpost.

STAVE V: THE END OF IT

YES! and the bedpost was his own. The bed was his own, the room was his own. Best and happiest of all, the Time before him was his own, to make amends in!

"I will live in the Past, the Present, and the Future!" Scrooge repeated, as he scrambled out of bed. "The Spirits of all Three shall strive within me. Oh Jacob Marley! Heaven, and the Christmas Time be praised for this! I say it on my knees, old Jacob; on my knees!"

He was so fluttered and so glowing with his good intentions, that his broken voice would scarcely answer to his call. He had been sobbing violently in his conflict with the Spirit, and his face was wet with tears.

"They are not torn down," cried Scrooge, folding one of his bed-curtains in his arms, "they are not torn down, rings and all. They are here—I am here—the shadows of the things that would have been, may be dispelled. They will be. I know they will!"

His hands were busy with his garments all this time; turning them inside out, putting them on upside down, tearing them, mislaying them, making them parties to every kind of extravagance.

"I don't know what to do!" cried Scrooge, laughing and crying in the same breath; and making a perfect Laocooen of himself with his stockings. "I am as light as a feather, I am as happy as an angel, I am as merry as a schoolboy. I am as giddy as a drunken man. A merry Christmas to everybody! A happy New Year to all the world. Hallo here! Whoop! Hallo!"

He had frisked into the sitting-room, and was now standing there: perfectly winded.

"There's the saucepan that the gruel was in!" cried Scrooge, starting off again, and going round the fireplace. "There's the door, by which the Ghost of Jacob Marley entered! There's the corner where the Ghost of Christmas Present, sat! There's the window where I saw the wandering Spirits! It's all right, it's all true, it all happened. Ha ha ha!"

Really, for a man who had been out of practice for so many years, it was a splendid laugh, a most illustrious laugh. The father of a long, long line of brilliant laughs!

"I don't know what day of the month it is!" said Scrooge. "I don't know how long I've been among the Spirits. I don't know anything. I'm quite a baby. Never mind. I don't care. I'd rather be a baby. Hallo! Whoop! Hallo here!"

He was checked in his transports by the churches ringing out the lustiest peals he had ever heard. Clash, clang, hammer; ding, dong, bell. Bell, dong, ding; hammer, clang, clash! Oh, glorious, glorious!

Running to the window, he opened it, and put out his head. No fog, no mist; clear, bright, jovial, stirring, cold; cold, piping for the blood to dance to; Golden sunlight; Heavenly sky; sweet fresh air; merry bells. Oh, glorious! Glorious!

"What's to-day!" cried Scrooge, calling downward to a boy in Sunday clothes, who perhaps had loitered in to look about him.

"EH?" returned the boy, with all his might of wonder.

"What's to-day, my fine fellow?" said Scrooge.

"To-day!" replied the boy. "Why, CHRISTMAS DAY."

"It's Christmas Day!" said Scrooge to himself. "I haven't missed it. The Spirits have done it all in one night. They can do anything they like. Of course they can. Of course they can. Hallo, my fine fellow!"

"Hallo!" returned the boy.

"Do you know the Poulterer's, in the next street but one, at the corner?" Scrooge inquired.

"I should hope I did," replied the lad.

"An intelligent boy!" said Scrooge. "A remarkable boy! Do you know whether they've sold the prize Turkey that was hanging up there?–Not the little prize Turkey: the big one?"

"What, the one as big as me?" returned the boy.

"What a delightful boy!" said Scrooge. "It's a pleasure to talk to him. Yes, my buck!"

"It's hanging there now," replied the boy.

"Is it?" said Scrooge. "Go and buy it."

"Walk-ER!" exclaimed the boy.

"No, no," said Scrooge, "I am in earnest. Go and buy it, and tell 'em to bring it here, that I may give them the direction where to take it. Come back with the man, and I'll give you a shilling. Come back with him in less than five minutes and I'll give you half-a-crown!"

The boy was off like a shot. He must have had a steady hand at a trigger who could have got a shot off half so fast.

"I'll send it to Bob Cratchit's!" whispered Scrooge, rubbing his hands, and splitting with a laugh. "He sha'n't know who sends it. It's twice the size of Tiny Tim. Joe Miller never made such a joke as sending it to Bob's will be!"

The hand in which he wrote the address was not a steady one, but write it he did, somehow, and went down-stairs to open the street door, ready for the coming of the poulterer's man. As he stood there, waiting his arrival, the knocker caught his eye.

"I shall love it, as long as I live!" cried Scrooge, patting it with his hand. "I scarcely ever looked at it before. What an honest expression it has in its face! It's a wonderful knocker!—Here's the Turkey! Hallo! Whoop! How are you! Merry Christmas!"

It was a Turkey! He never could have stood upon his legs, that bird. He would have snapped 'em short off in a minute, like sticks of sealing-wax.

"Why, it's impossible to carry that to Camden Town," said Scrooge. "You must have a cab."

The chuckle with which he said this, and the chuckle with which he paid for the Turkey, and the chuckle with which he paid for the cab, and the chuckle with which he recompensed the boy, were only to be exceeded by the chuckle with which he sat down breathless in his chair again, and chuckled till he cried.

Shaving was not an easy task, for his hand continued to shake very much; and shaving requires attention, even when you don't dance while you are at it. But if he had cut the end of his nose off, he would have put a piece of sticking-plaister over it, and been quite satisfied.

He dressed himself "all in his best," and at last got out into the streets. The people were by this time pouring forth, as he had seen them with the Ghost of Christmas Present; and walking with his hands behind him, Scrooge regarded every one with a delighted smile. He looked so irresistibly pleasant, in a word, that three or four good-humoured fellows said, "Good morning, sir! A merry Christmas to you!" And Scrooge said often afterwards, that of all the blithe sounds he had ever heard, those were the blithest in his ears.

He had not gone far, when coming on towards him he beheld the portly gentleman, who had walked into his counting-house the day before, and said, "Scrooge and Marley's, I believe?" It sent a pang across his heart to think how this old gentleman would look upon him when they met; but he knew what path lay straight before him, and he took it.

"My dear sir," said Scrooge, quickening his pace, and taking the old gentleman by both his hands. "How do you do? I hope you succeeded yesterday. It was very kind of you. A merry Christmas to you, sir!"

"Mr. Scrooge?"

"Yes," said Scrooge. "That is my name, and I fear it may not be pleasant to you. Allow me to ask your pardon. And will you have the goodness"—here Scrooge whispered in his ear.

"Lord bless me!" cried the gentleman, as if his breath were taken away. "My dear Mr. Scrooge, are you serious?"

"If you please," said Scrooge. "Not a farthing less. A great many back-payments are included in it, I assure you. Will you do me that favour?"

"My dear sir," said the other, shaking hands with him. "I don't know what to say to such munifi—"

"Don't say anything, please," retorted Scrooge. "Come and see me. Will you come and see me?"

"I will!" cried the old gentleman. And it was clear he meant to do it.

"Thank'ee," said Scrooge. "I am much obliged to you. I thank you fifty times. Bless you!"

He went to church, and walked about the streets, and watched the people hurrying to and fro, and patted children on the head, and questioned beggars, and looked down into the kitchens of houses, and up to the windows, and found that everything could yield him pleasure. He had never dreamed that any walk—that anything—could give him so much happiness. In the afternoon he turned his steps towards his nephew's house.

He passed the door a dozen times, before he had the courage to go up and knock. But he made a dash, and did it:

"Is your master at home, my dear?" said Scrooge to the girl. Nice girl! Very.

"Yes, sir."

"Where is he, my love?" said Scrooge.

"He's in the dining-room, sir, along with mistress. I'll show you up-stairs, if you please."

"Thank'ee. He knows me," said Scrooge, with his hand already on the dining-room lock. "I'll go in here, my dear."

He turned it gently, and sidled his face in, round the door. They were looking at the table (which was spread out in great array); for these young housekeepers are always nervous on such points, and like to see that everything is right.

"Fred!" said Scrooge.

Dear heart alive, how his niece by marriage started! Scrooge had forgotten, for the moment, about her sitting in the corner with the footstool, or he wouldn't have done it, on any account.

"Why bless my soul!" cried Fred, "who's that?"

"It's I. Your uncle Scrooge. I have come to dinner. Will you let me in, Fred?"

Let him in! It is a mercy he didn't shake his arm off. He was at home in five minutes. Nothing could be heartier. His niece looked just the same. So did Topper when he came. So did the plump sister when she came. So did every one when they came. Wonderful party, wonderful games, wonderful unanimity, won-der-ful happiness!

But he was early at the office next morning. Oh, he was early there. If he could only be there first, and catch Bob Cratchit coming late! That was the thing he had set his heart upon.

And he did it; yes, he did! The clock struck nine. No Bob. A quarter past. No Bob. He was full eighteen minutes and a half behind his time. Scrooge sat with his door wide open, that he might see him come into the Tank.

His hat was off, before he opened the door; his comforter too. He was on his stool in a jiffy; driving away with his pen, as if he were trying to overtake nine o'clock.

"Hallo!" growled Scrooge, in his accustomed voice, as near as he could feign it. "What do you mean by coming here at this time of day?"

"I am very sorry, sir," said Bob. "I am behind my time."

"You are?" repeated Scrooge. "Yes. I think you are. Step this way, sir, if you please."

"It's only once a year, sir," pleaded Bob, appearing from the Tank. "It shall not be repeated. I was making rather merry yesterday, sir."

"Now, I'll tell you what, my friend," said Scrooge, "I am not going to stand this sort of thing any longer. And therefore," he continued, leaping from his stool, and giving Bob such a dig in the waistcoat that he staggered back into the Tank again; "and therefore I am about to raise your salary!"

Bob trembled, and got a little nearer to the ruler. He had a momentary idea of knocking Scrooge down with it, holding him, and calling to the people in the court for help and a strait-waistcoat.

"A merry Christmas, Bob!" said Scrooge, with an earnest-ness that could not be mistaken, as he clapped him on the back. "A merrier Christmas, Bob, my good fellow, than I have given you, for many a year! I'll raise your salary, and endeavour to assist your struggling family, and we will discuss your affairs this very afternoon, over a Christmas bowl of smoking bishop, Bob! Make up the fires, and buy another coal-scuttle before you dot another i, Bob Cratchit!"

Scrooge was better than his word. He did it all, and infinitely more; and to Tiny Tim, who did NOT die, he was a second father. He became as good a friend, as good a master, and as good a man, as the good old city knew, or any other good old city, town, or borough, in the good old world. Some people laughed to see the alteration in him, but he let them laugh, and little heeded them; for he was wise enough to know that nothing ever happened on this globe, for good, at which some people did not have their fill of laughter in the outset; and knowing that such as these would be blind anyway, he thought it quite as well that they should wrinkle up their eyes in grins, as have the malady in less attractive forms. His own heart laughed: and that was quite enough for him.

He had no further intercourse with Spirits, but lived upon the Total Abstinence Principle, ever afterwards; and it was always said of him, that he knew how to keep Christmas well, if any man alive possessed the knowledge. May that be truly said of us, and all of us! And so, as Tiny Tim observed, God bless Us, Every One!

9 781951 872366